AF655942

Inormation Warfare
and
Cyber Security

Information Warfare and Cyber Security

R C Mishra

AUTHORSPRESS

Worldwide Circulation through Authorspress Global Network
First Published in 2003
by
Authorspress
Q-2A Hauz Khas Enclave, New Delhi-110 016 (India)
Phone: (0) 9818049852
E-mail: authorspressgroup@gmail.com
Website: www.authorspressbooks.com

Information Warfare and Cyber Security
ISBN 81-7273-143-4

Printed in India at Kensington Press

Preface

The spread of modern information technologies has brought about considerable changes in the global environment, ranging from the speed of economic transactions to the nature of social interactions to the management of military operations in both peacetime and war. The development of information technology makes it possible for adversaries to attack each other in new ways and with new forms of damage, and may create new targets for attack. As information technology has come to play an important and vital role in all sectors of society, security has become an essential component of information technology. The potential security threats and risks have to be carefully assessed in every situation, and it is absolutely vital that all concerned are made aware of the threats and risks that affect them, and over which they have control.

This book articulates on how warfare in the information age can devastatingly strike in an instant from across the globe, and that traditional military forces may be no match for superior technologists bent on stealing proprietary information, destroying the information infrastructure and thus the economy, or changing the military balance of power between adversarial nations. A comprehensive examination of the latest techniques and mechanisms, used to help protect internet and intranet access and communication services, are also well-discussed. It also explores the necessity to establish a strong operational relationship with both civil and military law enforcement organizations in order to be able to react quickly to potential cyber warfare.

R.C. Mishra

Contents

1

Technology Challenges in Information Warfare

The increasing flow of information, the evolution of the global economy, and the creation of the internet are all factors in creating the modern global village. The main actors in our society are fast becoming international corporations, rather than nations. It is plain that the changes in human society as a whole will entail changes in the way we wage war as well.

The Information Age empowers individuals with access, mobility, and the ability to effect change anywhere, instantaneously. It brings a new level of personalisation to our world that changes the value of consumer products and services. It promotes and enhances these rights by empowering the individual. Unlike television and radio, the Information Age digital communications allow on-demand programming

Spurred by Information Age technologies, our highly personalised social and political processes have become interconnected and non-linear, making it difficult to distinguish cause from effect and effect from cause. Our cyber-future will feature direct participation by the individual as opposed to group representation. As its value increases within our global economy, information is fast becoming a strategic national asset.

Through networking, the Information Age will allow more international economic alliances as well. The paradox is that networked economic alliances decrease the sovereignty of the nation-state. When the exchange of value occurs by electronic transmission rather than the transfer of products, trade policies become less important than the location of the network nodes. Governments that take the lead in understanding and building networks will gain enormous comparative advantages.

The Information Age has changed the nature of our economic and political interests and impacted on our national security interests. Unlike the Cold War era, political and economic interdependency in the Information Age requires cooperation and the open exchange of knowledge. Today, national objectives, other than the protection of the national information infrastructure, are not easily identifiable. Clearly, the emergence of global economic networks de-link national corporations from national markets and turn them multinational.

Economic security and prosperity in the Information Age are functions of a kind of equality between nations and firms. The more firms act internationally, the less they can be held to national accountability. Multinational firms play one nation-state against the other as they seek the greatest profit. Now trade agreements among sovereign nations are really inadequate when they do not include the concerns of global business organisations.

It is not difficult to show how the ways of security strategy change with the Information Age. For example, Information Age weapons are equallisers. They help small nations against large nations and favour the weak over the strong. Examples include Stinger missiles used by the Mujahideen against the Russians and computer viruses designed to invade individual weapon systems or an entire defence computer network. However, the real problem lies in the fact that today's breakthrough technologies in electronics, computer systems, software, and telecommunications come from the commercial marketplace and are available to anyone in the world. In broadest terms, information warfare (IW) is not new. It encompasses any hostile activity directed against our knowledge and belief systems.

Cyberwar, the newest subset of information warfare, needs no battlefield — it is fought in cyberspace. Cyberspace includes information itself, the communication nets that move it, and the computers that make it useful. Cyberspace can be influenced and at times dominated by anyone possessing inexpensive computers linked into existing global communication nets. The enemy may exploit global business organisations that produce cyber technology and determine the patterns of change. He may attempt to propagate waves of data big enough to crash the network by overloading network switches.

Under the microscope of world opinion formed by means of pervasive communication satellites, open warfare is no longer an option for sovereign nations to pursue their national interests. Cable News Network coverage can rapidly trigger a negative international response, as we have seen during the recent wars in Somalia and Bosnia. However, the Information Age offers a more subtle approach — waging a quiet war in cyberspace where digital fingerprints are hard, if not impossible, to trace. When information warfare enters and uses public cyberspace, collateral damage may be significant. Banking, finance, telecommunications, trade, travel, energy, and cultural systems are vulnerable. Misinformation and disinformation campaigns are easily mounted and hard to defend against.

The Information Age introduces at least three new concepts in the ways of strategy:

i) Information age weapons are equalisers and can negate the military principle of mass.
ii) Cyberwar needs no battlefield and therefore no specially trained military organisation—even civilians may participate.
iii) The initial offensive strike in a quiet cyberwar would be hard to detect and to defend against. It is also impossible to limit the cyberwar battlespace to purely military networks.

Compared with industrial age manufacturing, information-based industries can produce more with fewer resources, less energy, and less labour. Production runs of one are possible and even economical with intellectual capital (knowledge) encoded in software and used by smart machines. The result is an explosion of personalised products and services. Moreover, knowledge to inform people, coded as digital bits, can be turned into audio, video, or even graphics.

Unlike traditional means, knowledge is relatively cheap and easy to balance with ends and ways. Unlike conventional ways, cyberwar defies the military principle of mass. And its primary objectives are control and paralysis. Unlike the clearly articulated ends of Cold War security strategies, national objectives in a globally networked Information Age are more difficult to define and thus to achieve.

Information age military forces, evolving in their use of cyberspace, will follow the same path — first accommodating information technologies by incorporation, and next by re-inventing their processes and adapting their organisational structures. Success in future wars will require armed forces with open, adaptable organisations that can react more quickly to changes than can the competition. These organisations must easily re-configure to fill specific needs, saving time and money in the process. Such open organisations are not wedded to any one operating system; they can rapidly incorporate new Information Age technology.

Once the value of data is understood, knowledge derived from that data can be used offensively to increase an edge or defensively to reduce an edge held by an opponent. The ability to recognise the value of data and use this data to derive knowledge is the first step toward information dominance. Information dominance is achieved by transforming knowledge into capability. It is the ability to identify the vulnerabilities and centres of gravity of an enemy, or even a competitor or customer. It is the capability to reshape organisations and revise strategies based upon a systematic analysis of the opponent.

DIGITAL TOOLS FOR INFORMATION WARFARE

Information Technology (IT) plays a critical role in managing and operating nuclear-power plants, dams, the electric-power grid, the air-traffic-control system, and financial institutions. Large and small companies rely on computers to manage payroll, track inventory and sales, and perform research and development. Every stage of the distribution of food and energy, from producer to retail consumer, relies on computers and networks. A more recent trend is the embedding of computing capability in all kinds of devices and environments, as well as the networking of embedded systems into larger systems. The IT infrastructure can be conceptualised as four major elements:

i) the internet,
ii) the telecommunications infrastructure,
iii) embedded/real-time computing, and
iv) dedicated computing devices.

IT is clearly changing the landscape of political discourse and advocacy. It offers new and inexpensive methods for collecting and publishing information, for communicating and coordinating action on a global scale, and for reaching out to policy-makers. It supports both open and private communication. Advocacy groups and individuals worldwide are taking advantage of these features in their attempts to influence foreign policy. IT can also play a major role in the prevention, detection, and mitigation of terrorist attacks. By enabling wider awareness of critical information in the intelligence community, IT may facilitate the identification of important patterns of behaviour. Advances in information fusion, which is the aggregation of data from multiple sources for the purpose of discovering some insight, may be able to help in uncovering terrorists or their plans in time to prevent attacks. IT may also enable rapid and accurate identification of the nature of an attack and aid in responding more quickly.

Today critical information, both on and off the battlefield, flows from place to place by means of digital technology. It is not surprising that information warfare is fast becoming a hot topic in military circles. With the increasing digitisation of the battlefield it makes sense to find ways of protecting the computerised control of one's military apparatus, while at the same time coming up with the means to disrupt that of the other side.

Information warfare, both defensive and offensive, is not confined to the battlefield. In fact, it is a matter of far more urgency to the citizen than to the soldier. It is more than likely that both the victims and the perpetrators of information warfare will be found in the civilian sphere. This is because it is in our civilian lives that we are most vulnerable to the techniques of information warfare. It is to be expected that the military, concerned as it is with the continual need to protect its facilities and personnel from hostile action, will take all necessary precautions to guard its digital apparatus from outside interference.

Today, computers control our electric power supplies, run the national water system, control the air traffic into and out of the country, manage our bank accounts, and keep track of every aspect of our personal lives. All of these information systems are vulnerable, to one degree or another, to outside interference. In the past we have been fortunate in that the vulnerability of such systems has been less than the hacking talent of those who had most to gain by waging information war.

Terrorism is yet another example of how the focus of war has shifted toward civilian populations. The aim of terrorism is not to destroy the enemy's armed might, but to undermine his will to fight. The terrorist seeks to disrupt the daily life of his target nation by striking at the most vulnerable points in the society. Such vulnerable areas included transportation networks and public events, which insure good media coverage. By hitting the citizen just where he thinks he is safest, the terrorist causes the greatest confusion and loss of morale.

While the technology to operate and protect these networks is quite costly, the means required to attack them are relatively cheap. In the simplest case, one needs only a computer, a modem, and a willing hacker.

Due to the importance of the technical tools of IW and their fragility the possible contents of an IW techno-kitbag are listed below.

i) *Computer viruses:* A piece of code, or code fragment, designed to begin replicating itself when a host programme begins to run. Its objective is to erase data, software programmes, or memory in order to interrupt the action of the computer it infests.

ii) *Worms*: Instead of being just a code fragment, a worm is an entire programme in and of itself. The code begins to replicate as soon as it touches a computer system, not dependent on the start of execution of any other programme. Its aim is to eat up computer resources and/or delete data to result in a crippling effect on the host computer

iii) *Trojan horses*: A Trojan horse is a programme, or code fragment inside a programme, that performs a function unbeknownst to the user. It usually performs a simple task on the outside, while unleashing a virus or a worm on the inside. It can also perform information retrieval while performing a task, leaving no trace.

iv) *Logic bombs:* A logic bomb is used to release a virus, worm, or complete some other secret task. These are usually planted by a programmer or system developer.

v) *Trap doors:* The use of this is similar to a logic bomb. It is a secret way back into a system left by a programmer or designer. Unlike a logic bomb that executes, a trap door is merely an unknown security flaw.

vi) *Chipping*: This is the term for doing any of the above to the hardware of a system instead of to the software. One can build in circuitry to a chip that performs specific functions.

vii) *Machines and microbes*: Machines and microbes are tiny machines, like a small insect, that "eat" electronic circuits, oil, plastics, etc. If unleashed on a computer centre, the result would be total shut down.

viii) *Electronic jamming, HERF guns, and EM bombs*: These are all forms of electronic signal jamming. One can jam communications, stopping computer information flow; shoot radio signals at an electronic target to shut it down with a High Energy Radio Frequency (HERF) gun; or send out a high powered electromagnetic pulse, an EMP bomb.

ix) *Hitch-hiking*: This is a group of people, a subsection of hackers, that merely sit on the net and wait. They wait for any information and interesting code to go by and then hitch a ride with it, they follow and delete it, or they simply copy and steal it.

The following techniques will have to be considered as an IW operational security plan is built:

i) *Firewalls*: A limited gateway to the internet from a company or group. Only passwords and certain configurations can get in, and everything is checked for viruses, etc. Only privileged personnel, or personnel with certain system configurations can get out. If implemented correctly they can be useful.

ii) *Encryption*: This growing area of interest consists on coding data so that others cannot place bombs in or around it or read the data. This is growing more difficult as hackers and other groups become more efficient at breaking the codes.

MILITARY USE OF IW TOOLS

IT has always had a deep effect on organisations that conduct warfare and, in each case, innovations have forever changed the nature of warfare. Although it is expected that IT will continue to bring huge payoffs, military professionals cannot assume that the use of technology by itself will be the panacea for achieving risk-free operations. Digitisation promises to reduce the uncertainty and increase a warfighter's lethality; however, applying science to solve problems often leads to unanticipated new problems. Embracing digital technology may also bring accidental consequences that can damage and weaken military organisations.

There are three possible unintended consequences of IT that will affect military leaders' approach toward the art of war:

i) *Merging of operational and tactical levels of war*: The operational level serves as a link between strategic aims and tactical employment of forces. Digitisation unintentionally will have the effect of dismantling hierarchical structures and increasing the importance of the link between strategic and tactical levels. The traditional strategic, operational and tactical levels will gradually mutate into a blurry, flatter, two-tier hierarchy where the operational and tactical levels merge. It is not clear whether the effects of merging the levels are beneficial or detrimental to a theatre of operations.

ii) *General diminishing of a commander's prerogatives*: Since the future portends that threats will be less well defined, military missions will have more acute, direct political consequences that will demand a tighter reign on commanders. As a result of mass media coverage, civilian leaders will pressure military leaders for constant updates in order to maintain public support. It is quite possible that the initiative and boldness traditionally expected of American warfighters will be severely constrained by a superior's strong oversight. Digitisation, meant to give commanders greater autonomy, might actually strip commanders—especially those considered at the tactical level—of their individual prerogatives.

iii) *An increase in the fragility of the force*: As the services improve their lethality through digitisation, which also results in better situational awareness and quicker reaction times, the fragility of the force might increase. The new lack of robustness due to more complex electronic systems might negatively effect the ability of the force to quickly recover from the rigours of war. Issues concerning replacement of high-tech personnel casualties, availability of complex repair parts and ease at which long haul communications can be disrupted could all contribute dramatically to the future endurance of the joint digitised force.

With the help of information technology, joint commanders of the twenty-first century will be able to efficiently command and control geometrically greater battle spaces at a far greater tempo and confidence level. The amount of uncertainty will be less. The virtually seamless flow of information from the lowest echelons—conceivably individual battalions, ships or aircraft—gives joint commanders a significantly increased knowledge base from which to coordinate, synchronise, and employ forces. This knowledge will be shared nearly simultaneous throughout the chain of command. The force multiplying effect of shared information will be to achieve a greater coherence and unity of effort with significantly fewer casualties. Consequently, actions at every level will instantaneously effect the other and will have the affect of reducing the time between decisions.

The trend toward more powerful weapon systems will give rise to tactical elements being employed more often in direct support of strategic objectives. Situational awareness will permit the conduct of simultaneous offensive operations allowing the capability to convert tactical success immediately into decisive strategic results. In the pursuit of more decisive operations, a great shift in the power to make operational and tactical decisions at one echelon will occur. The desirability of this shift will depend on how senior leaders adapt to the greater responsibility.

A goal of joint digitisation is to provide a greater assimilation of more information into the warfighting process. This implementation goal will ultimately expand the strategic level's span of control with the streamlining of the operational chain of command. Today, military organisations are generally sized by how much one commander can effectively control. By design, each echelon's commander is better informed to make appropriate decisions concerning his responsibilities.

During the late 1980s and early 1990s, an evolution in business management led by the integration of information systems caused an increase in the span of control for a typical senior manager; this subsequently resulted in a flattening of the management structure. Likewise, digitisation will provide more senior leaders the information that will permit them to feel comfortable making more judgements that were traditionally left to operational and tactical commanders.

As technology increases the strategic echelon's span of control, there will be a predictable gravitation to coordinate tactical weapons at the highest possible level; thus, more pressure to flatten or merge the levels of war. Improved war-fighting capabilities which have increased the mobility, dispersion, lethality, and tempo will drive control measures at least to a joint theatre level. Centralised control is needed for synchronisation of combat power in order to conserve assets, and prevent fratricide and civilian collateral damage. Weapon systems could be enabled or disabled remotely whether they are on a ship, land or aircraft. It will be possible to control tactical fires and the manoeuvres of combat elements to optimise the direct obtainment of the strategic goal.

The significance for future military organisations is that traditional tactical and operational levels will have the same information and same battle space concerns. The need for separation based upon capability to command and control will likely cease to exist in the twenty-first century. The overall disadvantages of this merging has yet to form. How the senior leadership adapts and structures the resulting organisations will determine the magnitude of the drawbacks.

Digital technologies provide a tremendous capability; however, they must be weighted cautiously against their vulnerabilities. The use of digital technology has consequences that are paradoxical in nature. While it is true that the implementation of more advanced sensor-to-weapon systems will give better situational awareness, help minimise fratricide and better focus combat power, there is the concern whether the new electronic systems will have the resilience to absorb shocks and withstand perturbations associated with the realities of modern war. The more advanced the equipment the more complex it becomes. Generally, the more complex the system, the less reliable, and the harder or longer it takes to repair. A possible solution to the attrition issue is the use of redundancy in the digital architecture. Redundancy is not likely to protect the force as technology is being looked upon by our senior leaders to help mitigate the smaller force structure.

There are other compounding effects of attrition, such as the digital technologies dependence upon reliable communication architectures. It is the dependence and reliance of electronically synthesised data from widely dispersed systems that makes communications the most vulnerable segment. The greatest threat to the entire digitisation architecture is the lack of robust, redundant communications paths. Above the tactical level of war, it is anticipated for the twenty-first century that medium data rates for the military, as well as civilian satellite systems, will be vulnerable to jamming by today's low cost technology. Since digital communications demands are going to be predictably greater than their capacity, there will be no redundancy nor unused capacity. Even today, it is a doctrine not to normally keep communication equipment in reserve. Also, key communications equipment is subject to targeting through old-fashioned direct or indirect fires. An unsophisticated enemy sharpshooter could easily fire a well placed bullet and take out the feed to a critical satellite or a microwave antenna. This would effectively disrupt the digital architecture with devastating consequences to the command and control process.

Embracing digital technology offers a great deal to the warfighter. If the equipment envisioned for the future is developed and fully realised, the enhancement to Command and Control will dramatically streamline operations. For the future, technology will permit greater situational awareness that will reduce the commander's uncertainty and anxiety. It will certainly increase the warfighter's lethality through the ability to better focus and synchronise combat power.

The unintended consequences of this solution will be a challenge for future military leaders to understand. Leaders need to understand the impact upon the operational art of war that technology brings. Digital technology allows many advantages, but it is not without its soft intangible price. The possibility that the very strength that digital technology brings, situational awareness, may be the cause for trimming a commander's prerogatives.

TERRORIST AND IW TOOLS

As a technology for empowerment, the net benefits individuals and small groups with few resources as well as organisations that are large or well-funded. Although the media is a relatively new element in armed conflict, it is a weapon that terrorists have used from the outset. Indirectly, the internet may have also affected public support for the war, which in turn might have affected policy decisions made during the course of the conflict. There were three broad classes of activity: activism, hacktivism, and cyber-terrorism.

Activism, refers to normal, non-disruptive use of the internet in support of an agenda or cause. Operations in this area includes browsing the web for information, constructing websites and posting materials on them, transmitting electronic publications and letters through e-mail, and using the net to discuss issues, form coalitions, and plan and co-ordinate activities.

Hacktivism is the marriage of hacking and activism. It covers operations that use hacking techniques against a target's internet site with the intent of disrupting normal operations but not causing serious damage. Examples are web sit-ins and virtual blockades, automated e-mail bombs, web hacks, computer break-ins, and computer viruses and worms. The final category, cyber-terrorism, refers to the convergence of cyberspace and terrorism. It covers politically motivated hacking operations intended to cause grave harm such as loss of life or severe economic damage.

The internet is used extensively as a publication medium by hackers and terrorists. Hackers publish electronic magazines and put up websites with software tools and information about hacking, including details about vulnerabilities in popular systems and how they can be exploited, programmes for cracking passwords, software packages for writing computer viruses, and scripts for disabling or breaking into computer networks and websites. Virtually every terrorist group is on the web, along with a mishmash of freedom fighters, crusaders, propagandists, and mercenaries. Forcing them off the web is impossible, because they can set up their sites in countries with free-speech laws. The government of Sri Lanka, for example, banned the separatist Liberation Tigers of Tamil Eelam, but they have not even attempted to take down their London-based website.

Anti-government groups are establishing alliances and coalitions that might not have existed before the technology was introduced. Terrorists also use the internet to communicate and coordinate their activities. Back in 1996, the headquarters of terrorist financier Osama bin Laden in Afghanistan was equipped with computers and communications equipment. Egyptian "Afghan" computer experts were said to have helped devise a communication network that used the web, e-mail, and electronic bulletin boards. Hamas activists have been said to use chat rooms and e-mail to plan operations and coordinate activities, making it difficult for Israeli security officials to trace their messages and decode their contents.

Most of the e-mail was driven by an online advocacy campaign sponsored by the Libertarian Party. About 171,000 (83 per cent) of the e-mail messages were sent through the party's website. The party advertised its advocacy campaign in talk radio interviews and by sending a notice to its e-mail membership list. Indeed, many e-mail campaigns have been driven by non-government organisations.

Hacktivism includes electronic civil disobedience, which brings methods of civil disobedience to cyberspace. The hacktivism explores four types of operations: virtual sit-ins and blockades, automated e-mail bombs, web hacks and computer break-ins, and computer viruses and worms. Since hacking incidents are often reported in the media, operations in this category can generate considerable publicity for both the activists and their causes.

E-mail bomb is quite another to bombard them with thousands of messages at once, distributed with the aid of automated tools. The effect can be to completely jam a recipient's incoming e-mail box, making it impossible for legitimate e-mail to get through. Thus, an e-mail bomb is also a form of virtual blockade. Although e-mail bombs are often used as a means of revenge or harassment, they have also been used to protest government policies. In what some US intelligence authorities characterised as the first known attack by terrorists against a country's computer systems, ethnic Tamil guerrillas were said to have swamped Sri Lankan embassies with thousands of electronic mail messages. Web hacks and computer break-ins are extremely common, and targets include commercial and educational computers as well as government ones.

Most of the attacks, however, were probably not motivated by politics (hacktivism), but rather by thrills, curiosity, ego, revenge, or financial gain. Hacktivists have used computer viruses and worms to spread protest message and damage target computer systems. Both are forms of malicious code that infect computers and propagate over computer networks. The difference is that a worm is an autonomous piece of software that spreads on its own, whereas a virus attaches itself to other files and code segments and spreads through those elements, usually in response to actions taken by users.

It is extremely difficult, perhaps impossible, for an organisation to prevent all viruses, because users unwittingly open e-mail attachments with viruses and spread documents with viruses to colleagues. Although antiviral tools can detect and eradicate viruses, the tools must be kept uptodate across the enterprise, which may have tens of thousands of computers, and they must be installed and used properly. While viruses bearing political messages may not seem to pose a serious problem, an organisation hit by one may have to shut down services to eradicate it from its network. Viruses, especially those carrying destructive payloads, are a potentially potent tool in the hands of cyber-terrorists. Other tools of hacktivism, including computer network attacks, could likewise be put to highly destructive ends.

The term 'cyber-terrorism' to refer to the convergence of cyberspace and terrorism. Cyber-terrorism is the premeditated, politically motivated attack against information, computer systems, computer programmes, and data which result in violence against non-combatant targets by sub-national groups or clandestine agents. Politically motivated attacks that cause serious harm, such as severe economic hardship or sustained loss of power or water, might also be characterised as cyber-terrorism. Terrorist groups are using the internet extensively to spread their message and to communicate and coordinate action. However, there have been few, if any, computer network attacks that meet the criteria for cyber-terrorism.

The 1998 e-mail bombing by the internet Black Tigers against the Sri Lankan embassies was perhaps the closest thing to cyber-terrorism that has occurred so far, but the damage cause by the flood of e-mail, for example, pales in comparison to the deaths of 240 people from the physical bombings of the US embassies in Nairobi and Dar es Salaam in August of that year.

For a terrorist, it would have some advantages over physical methods. It could be conducted remotely and anonymously, it would be cheap, and it would not require the handling of explosives or a suicide mission. It would likely garner extensive media coverage, since journalists and the public alike are fascinated by practically any kind of computer attack. However, there are also drawbacks to terrorists using cyberweapons over physical ones. Since systems are complex, it may be harder to control an attack and achieve a desired level of damage. Unless people are injured, there is also less drama and emotional appeal. Further, terrorists may be disinclined to try new methods unless they see their old ones as inadequate.

The main effect of cyber-threats on foreign and domestic policy relates to defending against such acts, particularly attacks against critical infrastructures. At the international level, several countries, including the United States, have been addressing such issues as mutual legal assistance treaties, extradition, the sharing of intelligence, and the need for uniform computer crime laws so that cyber-criminals can be successfully investigated and prosecuted even when their crimes cross international borders, as they so often do. This effort is not focused on either cyber-terrorism or hacktivism, but rather addresses an array of actions that includes all forms of hacking and computer network attacks, computer and telecommunications fraud, child pornography on the net, and electronic piracy. It also covers state-sponsored cyberwarfare operations that use hacking and computer network attacks as a military weapon. Today, the evolution of cyber-threats has changed the situation dramatically.

A terrorist attack that involves the IT infrastructure can operate in one of three different modes. First, the attack can come in "through the wires" alone. Second, it can include the physical destruction of some IT element, such as a critical data centre or communications link. Third, the attack can rely on the compromising of a trusted insider who, for instance, provides passwords that permit outsiders to gain entry.

Compromised IT can have several disastrous effects: expansion of terrorists' opportunities to widen the damage of a physical attack; diminishment of timely responses to the attack; and heightened terror in the population through misinformation. The techniques to compromise key IT systems—e.g., launching distributed denial-of-service (DDOS) attacks against websites and servers of key government agencies at the federal, state, and local levels, using DDOS to disrupt agencies' telephone services and the emergency-response system, or sending e-mails containing false information with forged return addresses so they appear to be from trusted sources—are fairly straightforward and widely known. When an element of the IT infrastructure is directly targeted, the goal is to destroy a sufficient amount of IT-based capability to have a significant impact.

The internet could be seriously degraded for a relatively short period of time by a denial-of-service attack, but this is unlikely to be long lasting. The internet itself is a densely connected network of networks, which means that a large number of important nodes would have to be destroyed simultaneously to bring it down for an extended period of time. Destruction of some key internet nodes would result in slowed traffic across the internet, but the ease with which internet communications can be rerouted would minimise the long-term damage.

Another attack that would provide greater leverage is on the Domain Name System (DNS), which provides translation for the internet of domain names to specific IP addresses. There are a relatively small number of "root name servers" that provide these translation services, and while the DNS is configured to provide redundancy in case of accidental failure, it has some vulnerability to an intentional physical attack that might target all name servers simultaneously.

The telecommunications infrastructure of the public switched network is likely to be less robust. Although the long-haul telecommunications infrastructure is capable of dealing with single-point failures in such centres, the physical redundancy in that infrastructure is not infinite. An additional vulnerability in this telecommunications infrastructure is the local loop connecting central switching offices to end users-full recovery from the destruction of a central office entails the tedious rewiring of tens or hundreds of thousands of individual connections.

An electronic attack on a portion of the electric-power grid could result in significant damage, easily comparable to that associated with a local blackout. The real leverage of such an attack would likely be in amplifying the damage and costs associated with a physical attack on some other element of the critical infrastructure. In many of the same ways as embedded computing could be attacked, dedicated computers could also be corrupted in hard-to-detect ways. One possible channel arises from the extensive use of foreign IT talent among software vendors. Once working on the inside, perhaps after a period of years in which they act to gain responsibility and trust, it could happen that these individuals would be able to introduce additional but unauthorised functionality into systems that are widely used. Under such circumstances, their target might not be the general-purpose computer used in the majority of offices around the country, but rather the installation of hidden rogue code in particular sensitive offices.

Another channel arises from the connection of computers through the internet; such connections provide a potential route through which terrorists might attack computer systems that do provide important functionality for many sectors of the economy. Some disaster scenarios result in significant loss or damage that is all out of proportion to the actual functionality or capability destroyed. In particular, localised damage that results in massive loss of confidence in some critical part of the infrastructure could have such a disproportionate impact. Attacks that require execution over long periods of time are harder to mount and thus less likely than attacks that do not. Terrorist attacks can be sustained over time as well as occur in individual instances. If the effects of an attack sustained over time are cumulative, and if the attack goes undetected, the cumulative effects could reach very dangerous proportions. Since such an attack proceeds a little bit at a time, the resources needed to carry it out may well be less than in more concentrated attacks, thus making it more feasible. Plans that call for repeated attacks are less likely than plans that call for single attacks.

Terrorists are likely to concentrate their efforts where the impact is largest for the smallest expenditure of resources. For example, terrorists who want to create immediate public fear and terror are more likely to use a physical attack than an attack that targets IT exclusively. The reason is that the latter is not likely to be as cinematic as other attacks. The IT infrastructure can be a weapon used in an attack on something else as well as the target of an attack.

An attack using the IT infrastructure as a weapon has advantages and disadvantages from the point of view of a terrorist planner. It can be conducted at a distance in relative physical safety, in a relatively anonymous fashion, and in potentially undetectable ways. On the other hand, the impact of such an attack is indirect, harder to predict, and less certain. State sponsorship of terrorism poses threats of a different and higher order of magnitude, for a variety of reasons that include access to large amounts of financial backing and the ability to maintain an actively adversarial stance at a high level for extended periods of time.

SECURITY MEASURES

Cyber attacks can amplify the impact of physical attacks and lessen the effectiveness of emergency responses; reducing such vulnerabilities will require major advances in information and network security. The increasing levels of damage caused by cybercrime and the tendency to rely on the internet as the primary networking entity both suggest that the likelihood of severe damage through a cyber-attack is increasing. The evolution of the internet demonstrates increasing homogeneity in hardware and software, which makes it more vulnerable at the same time that it becomes more critical.

The issues raised by command, control, communications, and information (C3I) for emergency response for terrorist disasters differ from those for natural disasters for several reasons. Information fusion promises to play a central role in countering future terrorist efforts. In every case, information from many sources will have to be acquired, integrated, and appropriately interpreted to support decision makers.

Software flaws, lax procedures for creating and guarding passwords, compromised insiders, and non-secure entry points all lead to the conclusion that watertight perimeters cannot be assumed. Many advances in information and network security can improve computer systems' inherent reliability and availability, which are perennial concerns even under ordinary, non-threat conditions. Such dual-use capability could help generate broader interest in research and development on defensive technology, as well as motivate its incorporation into industry products.

Computer or telecommunications systems that contain sensitive information, or whose functioning is critical, must be protected at high levels of security. Firewalls are a minimal level of protection, but they are often bypassed for convenience. Truly vital systems may require an "air gap" that separates them from public networks. Likewise, communication links that must remain secure and available should use a private network.

In general, the IT infrastructure must be robust in the face of damage. Although incident management has been well studied, the IT requirements for such management do not appear to have been thoroughly conceived, even though in a disaster it is essential that IT systems provide for the capability to deliver information, interagency communication and coordination, and communication with those affected both within and beyond the immediate disaster area. Equipment must be deployed immediately to provide for appropriate communication to those responding to the situation, among the multiple agencies in the private and public sectors that are affected, and to and between those directly affected by the incident.

There are many options for helping to facilitate interoperable crisis communications among emergency-response agencies. Numerous computational and database facilities must be established to provide complete and real-time information to diverse constituencies whose information and communication requirements, security needs, and authorisations all differ. Furthermore, tight security is essential, especially if the incident is the result of a terrorist attack, because an active adversary might try to subvert the communications or destroy data integrity.

In addition, an atmosphere of crisis and emergency provides opportunities for hostile elements to overcome security measures that are normally operative under non-emergency circumstances; thus, another research area is how to build systems that permit security exceptions to be declared without introducing new vulnerabilities on a large scale. Efforts to coordinate communications are complicated by the fact that emergency response to a large-scale incident has many dimensions, including direct on-the-ground action and response, management of the incident response team, operations, logistics, planning, and even administration and finance.

In an emergency, extraordinary demands are placed on communications capacity. A disaster is likely to destroy some but not all of the communications infrastructure in a given area, leaving some residual capability. Meanwhile, the disaster provokes greater demands for communication from the general public. The result is often a denial-of-service condition for all, including emergency-communications services. The absence of a telephone dial tone in a disaster area is common because of increased demands. Even under high-traffic but non-emergency situations, cell-phone networks are sometimes unable to handle the volume of users in a given cell because of statistical fluctuations. Nor is the internet immune to such problems—congestion of shared internet links, including both last-mile and aggregated feeder links, can cause lockouts to occur on facilities that are still operational in the disaster area. One problem in this area is the management of traffic congestion and the development of priority overrides for emergency usage. Even today, many cellular networks allow the passing of text messages. The management of communications networks poses unique problems in a crowded, emergency disaster zone.

Security must be established rapidly from the outset, as the terrorists might try to mix among the first responders. It is also necessary to determine a means for temporarily suspending people's access to facilities, communications, and data without impeding the ability of those with legitimate need to use them. In a crisis, channels to provide information to the public will clearly be needed. Radio, television, and often the web provide such information today, but it is usually generic and not necessarily helpful to people in specific areas or with specific needs.

During an emergency, responders need information about physical on-the-ground conditions that is sufficiently fine-grained and accurate to be useful. It is virtually inevitable that no pre-existing sensor network will be in place to provide adequate information, so the deployment of sensors in response to a disaster is likely to be necessary. Depending on the nature of the emergency, sensor capacity would be needed to identify and track the spread of nuclear, chemical, or biological contaminants, characterise and track vehicular traffic, locate survivors, and find pathways through debris and rubble.

Therefore, technological solutions, such as embedded location sensors, are probably essential. Distributed sensor networks, either already in place or deployed in response to an incident, can be valuable information sources. While technologies like the Global Positioning System could also play a major role, airborne contaminants and equipment damage might render them ineffective.

Promising to play a central role in the future prevention, detection, and remediation of terrorist acts, "information fusion" is defined as the use of computer technology to acquire data from many sources, integrate these data into usable and accessible forms, and interpret them. Security checkpoints have become more important and more tedious than ever at airports, public buildings, sporting venues, and national borders. But the efficiency and effectiveness of checkpoints could be significantly improved by creating information-fusion tools to support the checkpoint operator in real time.

Intelligence agencies are routinely involved in information fusion as they attempt to track suspected terrorists and their activities, but one of their primary problems is managing the flood of data. There are well-known examples in which planned terrorist activity went undetected despite the fact that relevant evidence was available to spot it—the evidence was just one needle in a huge haystack.

Limitations of the current commercial technology include the inability to mine data that is a combination of text, image, video, and sensor information as well as the inability to incorporate the knowledge of human experts into the data-mining process. The area of language technologies has developed a wide variety of tools to deal with very large volumes of text and speech. A great deal of online information, in the form of text such as e-mail, news articles, memos, and pages on websites, is of potential importance for intelligence applications. The technologies for image and video processing tend to be domain-specific and often combine information from multiple modes.

In the event an attack does occur, whether against the IT infrastructure alone or against some physical part of the nation, IT may help to rapidly and accurately identify its nature, reduce its effectiveness, aid in responding to it, and enable a quicker and fuller recovery. Indeed, even if the IT infrastructure is not deliberately attacked, significant damage to it may be a consequence of an attack directed elsewhere, and in any event any significant attack will result in extraordinary demands for emergency communications being placed on it.

Information technologies for emergency response have not received a great deal of attention, though efforts in other contexts are intimately related to progress in this area. Information and network security is critical because of the potentially amplifying effect of attacks on IT when combined with attacks on the physical infrastructure, given the nation's increasing dependence on information technology.

IT for emergency response is essential because of the unfortunate reality that the probability of catastrophic terrorism cannot be reduced to zero; the ability to respond quickly and effectively to a catastrophic situation will always be needed. Information fusion is important in today's counter-terrorism efforts, where the essential problem is how to identify potential threats amidst enormous amounts of possibly relevant information; sophisticated techniques for filtering and processing this information are needed.

REFERENCES

Altschiller, Donald (ed.), *The Information Revolution*, New York: Wilson, 1995.

Anthony, Keith D., "Information Warfare: Good News and Bad News", *Military Intelligence* 23, January-March 1997, pp. 31-34.

Arquilla, John, and David F. Ronfeldt, *The Advent of Netwar,* Santa Monica, Calif.: RAND, MR-789-OSD, 1996.

Barac, Gregory G., "Interoperability: The Cornerstone of Information Warfare", *Strategy Research Project*, Carlisle Barracks: US Army War College, 12 April 1996.

Computer Science and Telecommunication Board, National Research Council, *Cyber Security Today and Tomorrow: Pay now or Pay Later*, National Academy Press, Washington DC, 2002.

Molander, Roger C., Andrew S. Riddile, and Peter A. Wilson, "Strategic Information Warfare: A New Face of War", *Parameters*, Autumn 1996, pp. 81-92.

Nye, Joseph, and William Owens, "The Information Edge", *Foreign Affairs*, Vol. 75, No. 2, March/April 1996.

Potter, David L., "Information Warfare: Malicious Software and Technology", *Military Intelligence* 23, January-March 1997, pp.34-37.

Richardson, Doug, "Information Warfare—New Threats and New Opportunities", *Asian Defence Journal*, no. 4, April 1997, pp.50-55.

Royal Canadian Mounted Police (RCMP), *Guide to Threat and Risk Assessment for Information Technology*, November, 1994.

Ryan, Donald E., Jr., "Implications of Information-Based Warfare", *Joint Force Quarterly*, no. 6, 1994-1995, pp.114-16.

Toffler, "Onward Cyber Soldiers", *Time Magazine,* August 21, Volume 146, No. 8, 1995.

2

Information Warfare: Conceptual Framework

Competition for information is as old as human conflict. It is virtually a defining characteristic of humanity. Nations, corporations, and individuals each seek to increase and protect their own store of information while trying to limit and penetrate the adversary's. Since around 1970, there have been extraordinary improvements in the technical means of collecting, storing, analysing, and transmitting information, since there is a 'technological revolution' sweeping through information systems and their integration into our daily lives leading to the term 'Information Age'. Information-related technologies concentrate data, vastly increase the rate at which we process and transmit data, and intimately couple the results into virtually every aspect of our lives.

The Information Age is also transforming all military operations by providing commanders with information unprecedented in quantity and quality. The commander with the advantage in observing the battlespace, analysing events, and distributing information possesses a powerful, if not decisive, lever over the adversary.

Information age warfare uses information technology as a tool to impart the combat operations with unprecedented economies of time and force. Ultimately, Information Age warfare will affect all combat operations. In contrast, information warfare, views information itself as a separate realm, potent weapon, and lucrative target.

One of the most intriguing ideas currently circulating in the defence community is the concept of information warfare (IW). It can refer to everything from computer viruses to 'smart' bombs, and encompass the activities of people as diverse as computer hackers and professional soldiers. For many defence analysts, it refers primarily the military application of computers and other information technologies. For other writers, however, IW is a much broader idea, relating to the emergence of 'Information Age' civilisation and the development of associated modes of political and social conflict which point toward the gradual erosion of nation-states and their monopoly of organised violence.

The 1991 Gulf War marked the early stages of a Military-Technical Revolution (MTR) which promises to transform the character of war as radically as did the advent of nuclear weapons 50 years age. Revolution in Military Affairs is a major change in the nature of warfare brought about by the innovative application of new technologies which, when combined with dramatic changes in Military Doctrine and Operational and Organisational Concepts, fundamentally alters the character and conduct of military operations. Since then, we have seen changes that enormously alter the face of military operations: the rebirth of regionalism, long submerged by superpower competition; the spread of democracy, with its sweet promise and bitter disappointment of enfranchisement; the difficulties of projecting just power from North America; and the evidence of technological efficiency in the form of precision delivery weapons and digital information processing and communication.

Revolution in military affairs matter principally for two reasons. First, being second best may lead to catastrophic loss in future wars. Since the only objective benchmark for determining the relative effectiveness of forces is unavailable in long periods of peace, there is great potential for asymmetries in combat effectiveness between militaries, observable only when the next war occurs. Secondly, as equipment lifecycles, especially for platforms, steadily grow to encompass decades, many of the principal weapons systems of 2025 will likely be designed and built in the next few years.

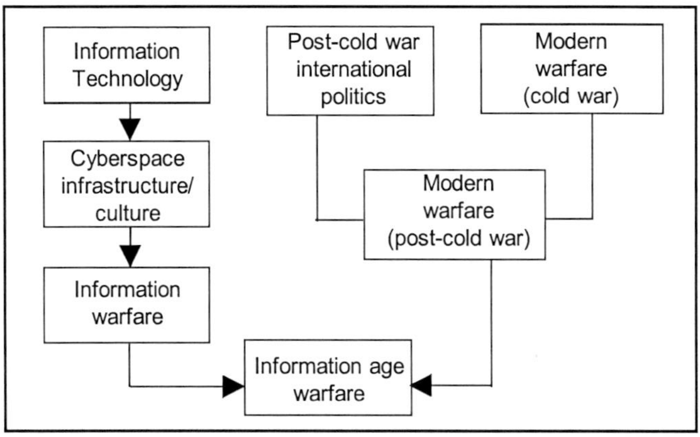

Figure 2.1: Schematic of information age warfare

Since militaries are stuck with force structures they choose for long periods, it is more crucial than ever to think about them now, in peacetime, about the revolutionary changes in the nature of war and the about what will matter in winning wars in 20 or 30 years. Today with the United States arguably the only superpower for the foreseeable future, one might ask why this issue is especially pressing.

The current rate of change suggests that state of the art in any technological context will be an extremely short-lived phenomenon, particularly with respect to the technologies that were key to the success of Desert Storm: space systems, telecommunication systems, computer architecture's, global information distribution networks, and navigation systems. Future revolutions will occur much more rapidly, offering far less time for adaptation to new methods of warfare. The growing imperative in the business world for rapid response to changing conditions in order to survive in an intensely competitive environment is surely instructive for military affairs.

The present revolution in military affairs entails a fundamental change in who, how, and, perhaps even why wars are fought. It is driven not only by new technologies but by new operational concepts, new tactics, and new organisational structures. The impact of the current confluence of social, political, economic, and technological forces on American society and armed forces may equal—or exceed—what occurred during the 1960s and 1970s during the turmoil associated with the war in Vietnam.

The current revolution in military affairs is characterised by four types of changes:

i) extremely precise;
ii) stand-off strikes;
iii) dramatically improved command, control, and intelligence;
iv) information warfare; and
v) non-lethality.

There are a number of benefits from harnessing the current revolution in military affairs and using it to build twenty-first century armed forces:

i) rejuvenating the political utility of military power;
ii) delaying the emergence of a peer competition;
iii) providing a blueprint for technology acquisition and force reorganisation; and
iv) inspiring conceptual, forward-looking thinking.

The current revolution in military affairs will have at least two stages. The first is based on stand-off platforms, stealth, precision, information domination, improved communications, computers, global positioning systems, digitisation, "smart" weapons systems, jointness, and use of ad hoc coalitions. The second may be based on robotics, non-lethality, pyscho-technology, cyber-defence, nano-technology, "brilliant" weapons systems, hyper-flexible organisations, and "fire ant warfare".

New technologies have spurred an entire new generation of war-fighting capabilities and, of equal importance, fundamentally altered the construct and performance of the modern nation-state. Discrete centres of gravity are giving way to diversification and interdependence in the modern nation-state. Information is the raw material that fuels productivity and power. Critical systemic nodes in the dynamic flow of commodities—consumables, services, and information—are at the same time increasingly obscure, strategically important, and tactically vulnerable. Fine grain analysis and precision targeting in both the conventional and non conventional sense of these nodes and their synergistic dependencies is the centerpiece of infrastructure warfare.

The primary elements of infrastructure warfare are:

i) The nation-state as a system of systems;
ii) Information as an instrument of power;
iii) Denial and deception;
iv) Urban infrastructure—the operational environment.

Though the concept of infrastructure warfare is certainly a step in the right direction, it has several shortcomings that need to be addressed. The conflicts of the new world disorder will be largely fought on geography in the Third World. Driven largely by the chimera of the Gulf War, images of centres of gravity and smart weapons overshadow the tawdry back-alley settings in which actual conflict will take place in the future. In reviewing the "lessons learned" of recent wars in the Third World—where 95 per cent of future conflicts will take place—a number of more accurate images appear:

i) The mix of forces facing each other has not been very different, regardless of the type of war being fought. Navies have been conspicuous by their absence or their modest role. Air forces have played a secondary role. Almost without exception, wars in the Third World have been won or lost by ground troops.

ii) The type of war has not necessarily determined the tactics used; in fact, it has blurred the differences between them. Furthermore, as the frequent oscillations in tactics and strategy suggest, both irregular and regular armies in recent years have shared much in term of their ability to implement offensive doctrine. With the exceptions of campaigns involving an industrialised power, it seems that the defence has become the most effective form of warfare in the Third World. With the exception of Israel and the war in Lebanon, none of the Third World combatants that have used an offensive doctrine has been able to effect a decisive breakthrough or cause the defenders to retire in disorder or retreat.

iii) The duration of recent wars have generally been protracted and have engaged large arrays of national and subnational forces. Most of the wars fought between regular lesser developed country army's have not been shorter.

iv) The involvement of external nation forces has been large. Of the wars fought between 1945 and 1976, 38 per cent were fought with foreign participation.

v) Since guerrilla wars pose particularly difficult challenges for governments, they represent a new and difficult form of conflict.

The infrastructure paradigm must address the Gray Area Phenomena (GAP). GAP is defined as threats to nation-states by non-states actors and non-governmental processes and organisations. The Gray Areas at once appear to be strikingly new and uncomfortably old. Just beyond the horizon of current events lie two possible futures—both of which look bleak. The first is the retribalisation of large swaths of humankind by war and bloodshed: a Lebanonisation of national states in which culture is pitted against culture, people against people, tribe against tribe—a jihad in the name of a hundred narrowly conceived faiths against every kind of globalisation and interdependence. The second is being borne by the onrush of technical, economic, and ecological forces that demand increased integration and uniformity.

The GAP consists of the following “arena’s of conflict”:

i) Ethno-religious-nationalistic conflicts;
ii) Weapons proliferation—both conventional and nuclear, biological and chemical;
iii) Conflict over scarce resources;
iv) AIDS and other infectious diseases;
v) The globalisation of organised crime;
vi) Drug trafficking;
vii) Economic warfare and conflict over technology;
viii) Emigration; and,
ix) Famine.

History has given evidence to the fact when some new technology brings mankind brightness, a shadow is cast simultaneously. Advanced electronic computers and information technology link society and the army to an integrated network; the result is very high efficiency and great fragility.

If information driven warfare means something new, it is the use of information as a substitute for traditional ways of fighting, rather than an adjunct to them. There are three ways that this might be achieved by:

i) the high technology equivalent of brute force;
ii) subversion; and,
iii) a new form of deterrence.

The evolution and ultimate "blurring" of military and civilian sectors came about in large part because of the growth in hardware and software. It was not so long ago, in the early 1960s, that the Pentagon provided the market for sophisticated electronics. Today, it makes up less than 1 per cent of that market. In many ways, the military is following the revolution, not leading it.

The speed of the growth and application of technology is clearly a concern for defence planners. While the US used some of the world's most advanced weaponry and technology in the Gulf War it also used a great deal of older technology, some of which dated back to the 1960s.

While at first glance it would appear that IW is most effective against adversaries with like technological capabilities and infrastructure—the top end of the IW target spectrum—it must be remembered that technology comes in two forms—high and appropriate—and it is the latter that will always defeat the former. Thus, the benefits of IW in arena's of conflict as found in the Gray Areas are a target-rich environment which must be pursued alongside the force on force approach.

Driving this revolution are advances in surveillance, communications, and information-processing technologies, which create the possibility of imbuing the information loop of warfare with unprecedented accuracy and speed, thereby achieving information dominance over less capable adversaries now. Information dominance, combined with cruise missiles and other precision weaponry, is expected to confer the ability to overwhelm virtually any opponent quickly, decisively and relatively bloodlessly. The key problem in this mode of warfare will be protecting one's own 'centres of gravity' or vulnerabilities while striking those of an enemy.

Military planners during the Cold War and inter-war periods faced the task of bringing known pieces of potential capability together in a fashion suited to an expected form of warfare against anticipated adversaries now. Under current conditions of rapid technological change and the emergence of new subnational and transnational players, however, such certainties are denied planners who cannot be sure about the form or participants that will characterise future wars.

The growing dependence of modern societies on computer-controlled information infrastructures is opening up new areas for unconventional warfare. Recent intrusions into the US civilian and military computer networks by hackers and criminals only hint at far more serious disruption that could be wrought by systematic electronic sabotage of national telecommunications systems power grids and financial institutions.

The advent of satellite-based global television broadcasting has created yet another arena for unconventional warfare. As was demonstrated in the Gulf War and the 1993 skirmishing in Somalia between UN forces and the clan warriors of General Aidid, live television coverage provides participants in armed conflicts with unprecedented opportunities to conduct military deception and shape the way distant audiences perceive events on the battlefield. Such "CNN Wars" are likely to become more common and to have disproportionately large political repercussions.

Information technologies are enlarging the venue of conflict from the traditional "battlefield" to computer networks, electronic databases, television screens, and other unconventional settings. They are also expanding opportunities for waging war through sabotage, terrorism, propaganda and similar clandestine means. One possible consequence is that it may be increasingly difficult to draw a clear line between war and other forms of conflict. Another is that distinctions between military and civilian practitioners of war may become progressively blurred.

Since modern high-tech armies are ill-suited to waging unconventional wars, they will either wither away or be transformed into paramilitary security forces. If, on the other hand, one accepts the premise that technology-based information superiority confers the ability to dominate any opponent, a military with this advantage should be able to prevail in unconventional wars. What is needed, however, is a conceptual framework that identifies strategies and requirements for achieving such dominance across the full spectrum of conflict.

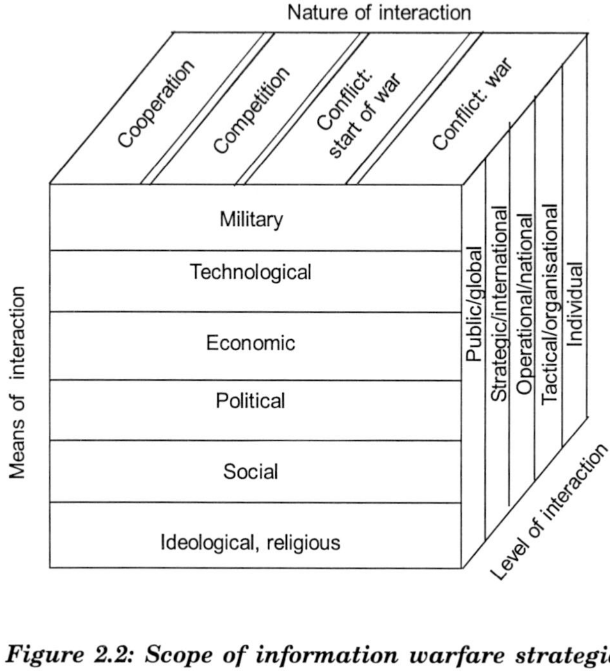

Figure 2.2: Scope of information warfare strategies

The US Department of Defence (DoD) has begun to expand its doctrine of Command and Control Warfare into the broader concept of Information Warfare (IW). According to a provisional DoD definition, IW consists of "actions taken to achieve information superiority in support of national military strategy by affecting adversary information and information systems while leveraging and protecting the information and information systems now." This formulation is intended to encompass military and non-military actions as well as defensive and offensive aspects. It also covers all levels of war from the tactical to strategic, and applies to both peacetime and wartime conditions.

FEATURES OF INFORMATION WARFARE

Information technology is more than just an enhancement of traditional military command and control, it changes the whole vision of military operations. Of course, very few missions can be accomplished solely with information means; information dominance without military means will not hold or take contested ground. Some of the defining features of IW are listed below:

i) *Low cost entry:* One of the consequences of both the rapid technological advance of information and the reductions in military budgets is concurrent adoption of both commercial technology and systems, and dependence on commercial information providers for equipment and services. Both of these are a source of fragility since the military systems not only share the same weaknesses and vulnerabilities of the civil systems, but increasingly depend on complex civil networks whose very complexity and concentration assume a peaceful, well-behaved environment. The vulnerabilities of these systems to "hackers" who may extract information, introduce inaccurate information, or introduce diseases such as viruses is a fragility of modern folklore. Combating these vulnerabilities is more than a matter of strengthening access security, but includes such measures as counter-hackers which conjures an image illustrating the changes in information warfare. The fragility of this feature is not limited to the information infrastructure. This technology also permits the proliferation of low-cost weapons either on a garage-industry level or nationally without substantial investment in lengthy and costly research and development efforts and infrastructure.

ii) *Blurred traditional boundaries*: One of the features of the modern world is a blurring of traditional boundaries. Part of this was telegraphed decades ago by the rise of multinational corporations, and part of it results from the end of the Cold War with regionalism emerging anew. Forces of regional, political, ethnic or religious determinism, perhaps frustrated by newly introduced democratic processes and the discovery of true minority status, have been unleashed.

iii) *Expanded role for perception management*: The proliferation of interest groups with political agendas has been accompanied by increases in communication availability. While the news media may not be naively susceptible to their propaganda, these groups have extensive opportunity for broadcast, notably the internet and fax machines. Indeed, the Information Age is characterised by more sources and quantities of information than can be digested. Coupled with the evolution and expansion of ethical and moral value ranges in the culture, a fragility of marshalling national will emerges. Increasing quantities of information and diversities of values combine to complicate consensus while solidity of value and purpose not only permit interest groups to act but to publicly rationalise their actions. Factor in distrust of large or established organisations, and the fragility only deepens. The connection between information visibility and disenfranchisement seems illogical, but it is the other side of the public discussion coin. Traditionally, information (media) visibility was limited and concentrated on perceived power groups. This drove small interest groups to compromise their tenets and goals to combine together to grow larger and gain information visibility. These groups then grew further because of their increased visibility and the marginal acceptability of their tenets and goals to newcomers. Accretion of the disaffected was assured by the visibility and the limited choices available.

iv) *Strategic Intelligence Inadequate*: Since nations developed, they have gathered intelligence on their potential and actual enemies. This task, once simple but large when the Soviet Union and the Warsaw Pact presented a monolithic threat, is now enlarged and complicated by the sheer diversity of actors including not only traditional nations but terrorists, drug cartels and political aspirants as well. Public repugnance of intelligence gathering is another source of fragility.

v) *Tactical warning and assessment*: Given the vulnerability of information networks to attack and the feasibility and efficacy of attacking logistic targets of national value and visibility, this lack of intelligence makes prevention more difficult and response more problematic. Sherlock Holmes could not solve mysteries without observations. Even with seemingly inexhaustible sources of information, it is hard to analyse these situations. Obviously, knowing something is an attack depends on recognising what attacks are possible and profitable.

vi) Building and sustaining coalitions is complicated. History teaches us that coalitions are difficult to construct and more difficult to maintain. Given the current environment of national and economic bloc commercial competition, regionalism, and the absence of a clearly defined and common enemy, modern coalitions are more problematic than ever.

TECHNICAL REALM OF INFORMATION WARFARE

Information warfare is an approach to armed conflict focusing on the management and use of information in all its forms to achieve a decisive military advantage in especially in the joint and combined environment. Information warfare is both offensive and defensive in nature—ranging from measures that prohibit the enemy from exploring information to corresponding measures to assure the integrity, availability, and interoperability of friendly information assets.

While ultimately military in nature, IW is also waged in political, economic, and social arenas and is applicable over the entire national security continuum from peace to war and from 'tooth to tail'. Finally, IW focuses on the command and control needs of the commander by employing state-of-the-art information technology such as synthetic environments to dominate the battlefield.

The technical realm of information based warfare can be split into two major areas: netwar and cyberwar.

i) *Netwar*: Netwar refers to information-related conflict at a grand level between nations or societies. It means trying to disrupt or damage what a target population knows or thinks it knows about itself and the world around it. A netwar may focus on public or elite opinion, or both. It may involve diplomacy, propaganda and psychological campaigns, political and cultural subversion, deception of or interference with local media, infiltration of computer networks and databases, and efforts to promote dissident or opposition movements across computer networks.

   In contrast to economic wars that target the production and distribution of goods, and political wars that aim at the leadership and institutions of a government, netwars would be distinguished by their targeting of information and communications. It will take various forms. Some may occur between the governments of rival nation-states. Other kinds of netwar may arise between governments and non-state actors. The non-state actors may or may not be associated with nations, and in some cases they may be organised into vast transnational coalitions. Some netwars will involve military issues, such as nuclear proliferation, drug smuggling and anti-terrorism, because of the potential threats they pose to international order and national security.

Netwars are not real wars, traditionally defined. But netwar might be developed into an instrument for trying, early on, to prevent a real war from arising. Netwar can be broken into three main categories: personal, corporate, and global. But protecting yourself from someone who genuinely wants to conduct information war against you is nearly impossible.

Corporations are subject to a barrage of information security problems to an even greater extent. The stealing of company secrets is a new form of economic war that is plaguing many companies. It is also possible for one company to release false findings that indicate that a competitor has a poor or dangerous product. IW spawned misinformation—a fertile area for denial and deception techniques—are very difficult to combat and correct. Finally, on the global level, netwar can be waged against industries, economies, nations, or non-state groups. The impact at the global level can be much more widespread and all threatening than that of the personal or corporate levels of netwar.

ii) *Cyberwar*: Cyberwar refers to conducting military operations according to information-related principles. It means disrupting or destroying information and communications systems. This form of warfare may involve diverse technologies, notably for command and control, for intelligence collection, processing and distribution, for tactical communications, positioning, identifying friend-or-foe, and for "smart" weapons systems, to give but a few examples. Cyber war has broad ramifications for military organisation and doctrine. Moving to networked structures may require some decentralisation of command and control. But decentralisation is only part of the picture. The new technology may also provide greater 'topsight', a central understanding of the big picture that enhances the management of complexity. It may imply developing new doctrines about the kinds of forces needed, where and how

> to deploy them, and how to strike the enemy. How and where to position what kinds of computers, sensors, networks and databases may become as important as the question once was for the deployment of bombers and their support functions.

On both sides of the war, the key to good protection and offence is good software to run the systems, encode the data, and peck holes in others data. The vital link for the information and the technology is software, which relies heavily upon implanted logic. The newest and brightest theories and concepts of logic centre around what is called 'fuzzy logic'. The name fuzzy logic makes one think of a system that is inexact, but that is not the case, instead it has an infinite exactness.

Fuzzy logic expands our normal computer principle of 0 or 1, true or false, and in the place of this is infinite degrees between 0 and 1. Fuzzy logic is used every day in the development of everything from smart washers to train systems in Japan. With a smart washer, you merely press a start button and the machine figures the cycle, how much detergent, and the water use; the logic train systems are smooth as silk, quick, and always on time.

IW has become central to the way nations fight wars. Military operations make special demands on information functions in seeking to give the commander an information advantage. The commander with better information holds a powerful advantage over his adversary. At the grand strategy level, nations seek to acquire, exploit, and protect information in support of their objectives.

This exploitation and protection can occur in the economic, political, or military arenas. Knowledge of the adversary's information is a means to enhance our capabilities, degrade or counteract enemy capabilities, and protect our assets, including the information. This is not new. The struggle to discover and exploit information started the first time one group of people tried to gain advantage over another.

IW consists of targeting the enemy's information and information functions, while protecting our own, with the intent of degrading his will or capability to fight. It can be defined as any action to protect our information functions, regardless of the means. Hardening and defending the switching facility against air attack is information warfare. So is using an anti-virus programme to protect the facility's software. It is a means, not an end, in precisely the same manner that air warfare is a means, not an end. Militaries have always tried to gain or affect the information required for an adversary to effectively employ forces.

Past strategies typically relied on measures such as feints and deception to influence decisions by affecting the decision maker's perceptions. Since these strategies influenced information through the perception process, they attacked the enemy's information indirectly. That is, for deception to be effective, the enemy had to observe the deception, analyse the deception as reality, and act upon the deception according to the deceiver's goals. However, modern means of performing information functions give information added vulnerability: direct access and manipulation. Modern technology now permits an adversary to change or create information without relying on observation and interpretation. Here is a short list of modern information system characteristics creating this vulnerability:

i) concentrated storage,
ii) access speed,
iii) widespread information transmission, and
iv) the increased capacity for information systems to direct actions autonomously.

Intelligent security measures can reduce, but not eliminate, this vulnerability; their absence makes it glaring. Militaries are not inclined to trust their success to the fortunes of war. So they must direct information warfare efforts to more than just targeting an adversary's information: they must also defend. The integrity of military information functions, as well as the information itself, bears heavily and directly on the success of military operations.

The Information Age has provided new and practical means to deny, exploit, corrupt, or destroy information, as well as the vulnerabilities to make those attacks possible. Information attack directly corrupts information without visibly changing the physical entity within which it resides.

Constrained by the definition of information, it is limited to directly altering data or instructions. It is, therefore, just another means of conducting information warfare, one whose immediate effects do not include visible changes to the entity within which the information resides. After being subjected to information attack, an information function is indistinguishable from its original state except through inspecting its data or instructions.

There are two ways to influence the adversary's information functions:

i) indirectly and
ii) directly.

Indirect information warfare affects information by creating phenomena, which the adversary will perceive, interpret, and act upon. Military deception, physical attack, and OPSEC traditionally achieved their ends indirectly.

For example, the goal of deception is to cause the adversary to make incorrect decisions; deception does this by creating an apparent reality. Generally, this entails creating phenomena for the enemy to observer. Success, however, depends on several conditional events: the adversary actually observes the phenomenon, thereby turning it into data; analyses it into the desired information; and acts upon the information in the desired manner. Direct information warfare affects information through altering its components without relying on the adversary's powers of perception or interpretation. Information attack acts directly upon the adversary's information.

Since nearly all modern information functions are themselves controlled by information, information attack may be directed against most information functions. Direct information warfare, the point of information attack, acts on the adversary's information without relying on the adversary's collection, analysis, or decision functions.

The difference between indirect and direct information warfare applications is:

i) *Indirect information warfare:* Using military deception, we could construct fake runways and parking areas, and generate enough other activities to present a convincing image. We rely on the adversary to observe the pseudo combat operation and interpret it as real. Only then does it become the information we want the adversary to have.

ii) *Direct information warfare:* Conversely, if we use information attack to create the pseudo combat wing in the adversary's store of information, the result—deception—is precisely the same. But the means to that result, never mind the resources, time, and uncertainty, are dramatically different.

The defensive side of information warfare security measures aimed at protecting information prevents an adversary from conducting successful information warfare against our information functions.

Current security measures are typical means of preventing, detecting, and subverting an adversary's indirect actions on military information functions. Future security measures must evolve as information technology advances. Consequently, new measures will likely take forms entirely different from today's security measures, rooted as they are in previous security requirements.

As military operations become more technologically sophisticated, they become more technologically dependent. Information warfare is very important to military operations, because it offers important means to accomplish the missions. But the Information Age changed the information realm's characteristics so that widespread military operations within it became practical. Information warfare is the means defined by the environment to execute military missions.

There are three objectives of IW:

i) Control the information realm so we can exploit it while protecting military information functions from enemy action,
ii) Exploit control of information to employ information warfare against the enemy, and,
iii) Enhance overall force effectiveness by fully developing military information functions.

The focus of information warfare is any information function, whether it is a refinery's control system, or a telephone switching station. Command and control warfare (C2W) only addresses activities directed against the adversary's ability to direct the disposition and employment of forces, or those which protect the friendly commander's ability to do so.

IW not only attacks the C2 process, but it also attacks the enemy's combat power itself. Conversely, by definition, C2W is not associated with reducing or nullifying the ability or desire of combat units to execute their orders. Tactical psychological operations and electronic countermeasures self-protection hinder the ability of units to execute orders. But they in no way affect commanders' ability to issue orders to those units, nor their ability to receive those orders. Information warfare might be a means to conduct any mission the services already conduct and the services are best positioned to choose the best means for their ends. Each service has its own unique operational demands.

REFERENCES

Biddle, Stephen, "Assessing Theories of Future Warfare", paper presented to the 1997 Annual Meeting of the American Political Science Association, August 29, 1997, pp. 24–33.

Cohen, Eliot, "A Revolution in Warfare", *Foreign Affairs*, Vol. 75, No. 2, March–April 1996, pp. 46–48.

Dearth, Douglas, and Charles Williams, "Information Age/Information War", in Campen, Dearth, and Goodden, 1996.

Department of the Air Force, *Cornerstones of Information Warfare*, Washington, D.C.: Department of the Air Force, 1995.

Definitions for the Discipline of Information Warfare and Strategy, Washington, D.C.: School of Information Warfare and Strategy, National Defense University.

Friedman, George, and Meredith Friedman, *The Future of War: Power, Technology and American World Dominance in the 21st Century,* New York: St Martin's Press, 1997.

Harknett, Richard J., "Information Warfare and Deterrence", *Parameters*, Autumn 1996, pp. 93–107.

Libicki, Martin C., *What Is Information Warfare?* Washington, D.C.: National Defense University, 1995.

_______________ , *Defending Cyberspace and Other Metaphors*, Washington, D.C.: NDU Books, 1997.

Molander, Roger C., Andrew S. Riddile, and Peter Wilson. *Strategic Information Warfare: A New Face of War*, Santa Monica, Calif.: RAND, MR-661-OSD, 1996.

Murray, Williamson, "Thinking about Revolutions in Military Affairs", *Joint Forces Quarterly,* Summer 1997, pp. 60–76.

_______________ , Allan R. Millett, (ed.), *Military innovation in the Interwar Period*, New York: Cambridge University Press, 1996.

Nichiporuk, Brian, and Carl H. Builder, *Information Technologies and the Future of Land Warfare*, Santa Monica, Calif.: RAND, MR-560-A, 1995.

Ryan, Donald E., Jr., "Implications of Information-Based Warfare", *Joint Force Quarterly*, no. 6, 1994-1995, pp.114-16.

Toffler, Alvin, and Heidi Toffler, *War and Anti-War: Survival at the Dawn of the 21st Century*, Boston: Little, Brown, 1993.

Tsymbal, V. I., "Concepts of Information Warfare", a speech presented at the conference on Evolving Post–Cold War National Security Issues, held in Moscow, September 12–14, 1995.

Widnall, Sheila, and Richard Fogleman, "Cornerstones of Information Warfare", U.S. Air Force White Paper, 1996.

3

Methods, Tools and Practices

The information revolution is altering the nature of conflict across the spectrum. We call attention to two developments in particular. First, this revolution is favouring and strengthening network forms of organisation, often giving them an advantage over hierarchical forms. The rise of networks means that power is migrating to non-state actors, because they are able to organise into sprawling multi-organisational networks more readily than can traditional, hierarchical, state actors. Second, as the information revolution deepens, the conduct and outcome of conflicts increasingly depend on information and communications.

Networks come in three major typologies: chain, hub, and all-channel. There are also complex combinations and hybrids involving myriad nodes and links—as in "spider webs", as well as in centre/periphery and clique networks. There are also designs that amount to hybrids of networks and hierarchies. The strongest networks will be those in which the organisational design is sustained by a winning story and a well-defined doctrine, and in which all this is layered atop advanced communications systems and rests on strong personal and social ties at the base. For practitioners trying to organise a new network or adjust one that already exists, various options may merit consideration and their assessment should assure that all the organisational, narrative, doctrinal, technological, and social levels are well-designed and integrated.

Networked organisations share three basic sets of features. First, communication and coordination are not formally specified by horizontal and vertical reporting relationships, but rather emerge and change according to the task at hand. Similarly, relationships are often informal and marked by varying degrees of intensity, depending on the needs of the organisation. Second, internal networks are usually complemented by linkages to individuals outside the organisation, often spanning national boundaries. Like internal connections, external relationships are formed and wind down according to the lifecycle of particular joint projects. Third, both internal and external ties are enabled not by bureaucratic fiat, but rather by shared norms and values, as well as by reciprocal trust.

Today, networks are one of the most common forms of social organisation. They are simultaneously pervasive and intangible, ubiquitous and invisible, everywhere and nowhere. Networks are not an exclusive organisational form and often exist within more traditional hierarchical structures, cutting through divisions based on specialisation or rank. It is also possible to have networks in which hierarchical organisations are key participants. Networks are also an important complement to markets, making them more efficient, reducing transaction costs, and providing increased opportunities for both buyers and sellers. These characteristics—their pervasiveness, their capacity to coexist both within and outside hierarchies, their ability to make markets more efficient by facilitating directed flows of information and commodities—give networks an elusive quality. Networks vary in size, shape, membership, cohesion, and purpose. Networks can be large or small, local or global, domestic or transnational, cohesive or diffuse, centrally directed or highly decentralised, purposeful or directionless.

A specific network can be narrowly and tightly focused on one goal or broadly oriented toward many goals, and it can be either exclusive or encompassing in its membership. Networks facilitate flows of information, knowledge, and communication as well as more-tangible commodities. As communications have become cheaper and easier, networks have expanded enormously. Indeed, technological networks facilitate the operation of larger and more-dispersed social networks and can even act as a critical force multiplier for certain kinds of social networks.

Specify critical roles in criminal networks, bearing in mind that there are network roles that relate to the functioning of the network and substantive roles related specifically to the nature of the criminal enterprise. In some cases, these two roles might overlap; in others, however, they will be quite distinct. Highlight and assess the operations of criminal networks. A network can be understood very simply as a series of nodes that are connected. The nodes can be individuals, organisations, firms, or computers, so long as they are connected in significant ways.

Social network analysis originated in several fields, including anthropology, sociology, and social psychology. Accordingly, social network analysis examines such issues as the importance or prominence of particular individuals in the network; the concept of centrality, i.e., the individual in the network with the most-or most important-ties to other actors; the notions of closeness and distance based on communication paths among the actors in the network; the notion of cohesive subgroups, that is, subsets of actors among whom there are relatively strong, direct, intense, frequent, or positive ties; the extent to which the relationships and transactions within it are regulated by explicit or tacit rules; and the number and diversity of actors within the network. The network-based organisations are capable of superior performance than are more traditionally structured hierarchical organisations, especially in terms of adaptability to changes in their environment.

Networks in business has emerged in response to the limitations, rigidities, and inefficiencies associated with strict hierarchical structures, the need to exploit globalisation through partnerships and strategic alliances. It has also emerged out of a recognition that understanding the opportunities provided by "structural holes" can be critically important for the success of a business in a competitive environment. The notion of business networks has been developed most explicitly, however, in the concept of the virtual corporation and its dependence on what are sometimes termed "agile networks". Such notions place considerable emphasis on flexible internal communication networks; connections to other organisations; shared interests in obtaining certain outcomes; the need to respond rapidly to external opportunities and challenges; the capacity for environmental scanning, rapid information-processing, and quick decisionmaking; and the capacity of the organisation to learn and adapt.

CRIMINAL NETWORKS

Although networks are an important, and somewhat neglected, form of criminal organisation, they are not the sole or exclusive form. First, a network can be created and directed by a core of organisers who want to use it for specific purposes or it can emerge spontaneously as a mechanism to add efficiency to the functioning of a market. The Colombian cocaine trade in the 1980s and early 1990s was very much a directed network—at least at the core—which came into existence to transport cocaine to the United States. The heroin trade from South-east Asia, in contrast, is far more of a transaction network, in which brokers play a critical role at almost every stage of the process. Producers supply heroin to independent distributors, and it is then passed along a chain of brokers until it reaches the retail market. Second, networks can range from small, very limited associations at the local level to transnational supplier networks that move a variety of goods, either licit or illicit—or even bcth—across national borders. Third, networks can be highly structured and enduring in nature or they can be loose, fluid, or amorphous in character, with members coming and going according to particular needs, opportunities, and demands. Some individuals or even small organisations will drift in and out of networks when it is convenient for them to do so. Other networks will have a more enduring membership. Last, networks can be focused very narrowly on a single purpose or on the supply of a single product, or they can supply a broader range of illegal products or engage in more diverse criminal activities.

In contrast, Russian and Chinese criminal organisations have a very diverse portfolio of criminal activities, trafficking in drugs, stolen cars, arms, prostitution, antiquities, and endangered species, yet also engaging in various forms of extortion and financial fraud. Whatever their precise characteristics, networks provide criminals with diversity, flexibility, low visibility, durability, and the like. Networks can often operate clandestinely. The more visible a criminal enterprise the more likely it is to be attacked by law enforcement.

One of the most significant points about networks, however, is that they are not immediately and obviously visible. Criminal networks can hide behind various licit activities, can operate with a lower degree of formality than other types of organisation, and can maintain a profile that does not bring them to the attention of law enforcement.

Many criminal networks are inherently dispersed, with the result that they do not provide obvious centres of gravity or loci for law enforcement attacks. Lacking a physical infrastructure or a large investment of sunk costs that would add significantly to their vulnerability, networks can also migrate easily from areas where risks from law enforcement are high to areas where the risks are much lower. Criminal networks, especially when they are transnational in character, can exploit differences in national laws and regulations by engaging in what might be termed jurisdictional arbitrage.

Throughout the 1990s, for example, criminals from the former Soviet Union flooded into Israel, exploiting both the law of return and the lack of anti-money laundering measures. In some cases, money from Russia was used in Israel to buy up virtually bankrupt businesses that would then start to make "profits" that flowed back to Russia. In some instances transnational criminal organisations also create jurisdictional confusion, making it difficult for any single nation's law enforcement agencies to act effectively against them.

In network structures, it is easier to create redundancies than it is in more formal and rigid organisations, so that even if part of the network is destroyed it can still operate. Furthermore, degradation of a network does not necessarily lead to its demise. Networks are very resilient and can easily be rebuilt.

The network core is characterised by dense connections among individuals who, in the case of a directed network, provide the steering mechanism for the network as a whole. Usually the originators of the criminal enterprise, the core members initiate specific criminal activities, arbitrate disputes, and provide direction. Their relationship is often underpinned by bonding mechanisms that help to create high degrees of trust and cohesion. If network cores exhibit strong collective identities, cohesion does not necessarily enhance—and can actually reduce—the capacity to obtain information and "mobilise resources from the environment".

These characteristics play a critical role in networks, exhibiting and exploiting "the strength of weak ties". In effect, the periphery allows the network to operate at a far greater distance—both geographically and socially—than would otherwise be the case, facilitating more extensive operations, more diverse activities, and the capacity to carry out effective intelligence collection. For criminal networks, this capacity is critical, because it allows them to anticipate and thereby to neutralise many law enforcement initiatives.

If criminal networks usually have early warning mechanisms that provide the first line of defence against law enforcement, there are also additional defensive mechanisms that can be integrated very effectively into their network structures.

Compartmented networks are good at protecting not only the core membership but also information that could compromise criminal operations or the integrity of the network. Criminal networks compartmentalise knowledge and information, making it difficult for law enforcement to have more than localised effects on their operations. For the most part, however, networks are very good at self-protection. Electronic surveillance is also highly problematic since many of the networks use unfamiliar languages or dialects.

An additional problem is that criminal networks based on ethnicity are generally located in ethnic communities that offer cover, concealment, and a constant supply of recruits. This is an important factor, for example, in explaining the success of Turkish drug trafficking organisations, and more recently Albanian criminal networks in Western Europe. Even distinctively ethnic networks are not exclusive in their collaboration.

Criminal networks come together with one another when it is convenient or beneficial for them to do so without this being a threat to their identity or *raison d'etre*. Connections among different criminal networks became a major feature of the organised crime world during the 1990s. Italian and Russian criminal networks have also forged cooperative relationships, while Colombian and Russian criminals have been meeting in various Caribbean islands to engage in guns-for-drugs deals.

Some of the more traditional criminal organisations, such as the Sicilians, are also reliant on networks of cooperation to ply their criminal trade. In short, the internal flexibility of network organisations is mirrored in the capacity of criminals to form and operate flexible alliances and other cooperative ventures. Indeed, network structures facilitate cooperation among criminal enterprises in the same way they facilitate cooperation in the licit business world. Criminal networks are also able to draw on a whole set of support structures, whether through acts of paternalism in the community or through more strictly financial considerations. Among the support structures are groups that provide false documentation, front companies, transportation, and a financial infrastructure that can be used to move the proceeds of crime.

The creation of false documents facilitates the movement of various kinds of contraband and people and offers an extra layer of protection for those involved in criminal activities. Another closely related advantage of criminal networks is their capacity to flow around physical barriers and across legal or geographical boundaries. Networks transcend borders and are well-suited for business operations in a world where responding to the opportunities and challenges posed by globalisation has become an imperative. The capacity to cross national borders creates several advantages for criminal networks. It enables them to supply markets where the profit margins are the largest, operate from and in countries where risks are the least, complicate the tasks of law enforcement agencies that are trying to combat them, commit crimes that cross jurisdictions and therefore increase complexity, and adapt their behaviour to counter or neutralise law enforcement initiatives. One important boundary crossing, of course, is that between the criminal world and the "upper world."

Networks provide access to people with specific resources, which create mutually advantageous information benefits and exchange relationships. This is as relevant to organised crime as to business and helps to explain why criminal organisations extend their networks into the licit world. Further, extending a network into government provides access to both information and power. For criminal networks, spanning structural holes is particularly beneficial when it also involves crossing from one domain into another. By crossing from the underworld into the worlds of government, business, and finance, criminal networks not only identify and exploit new criminal opportunities, but also enhance their capacity to protect existing activities and opportunities.

For criminal organisations involved simply in theft, for example, the critical node is the person who can fence the goods, who in effect transfers them from the criminal network back into the world of legitimate business and commerce. At a more sophisticated level are found the lawyers, accountants, bankers, and other financial professionals who help criminals both to conceal and to invest their profits. This facilitates the flow of criminal proceeds back into the legitimate financial system, where it rapidly becomes indistinguishable from money that has been obtained by legal means.

In short, criminal organisations extend their reach by co-opting individuals and organisations in ways that facilitate, enhance, or protect their activities. The corruption networks they create are dynamic rather than static, increasing in significance as corrupted officials become more senior. In these circumstances, the exchange relationship between them becomes much more substantial in terms both of the favours done by the official and the pay-offs provided by the criminal. While the official is not part of a criminal enterprise, he has become a vital node in a criminal network, providing important services including timely intelligence about law enforcement initiatives.

Criminal networks—apart from the core–are based largely on loose coupling. Even if some parts of the network are destroyed, the effects are limited since other parts are left intact. In a loosely coupled network, knock-on or cascading effects are limited and damage to one part of the network does not undermine the network as a whole. Loose coupling also preserves more diversity, in response offering considerable latitude in the decision of which parts of the network should respond, in what manner and in what location. Criminal networks often develop certain forms of redundancy that facilitate recovery if part of the network is degraded or damaged. In legitimate business, redundant contacts in networks—and indeed redundancy in general—are generally seen as wasteful and inefficient.

For criminal networks, such costs are greatly outweighed by the benefits of redundancy in the face of attack and degradation by law enforcement. The more redundancy in the network, the more options there are to compensate for law enforcement successes whether in finding new ways of moving illicit commodities to the market or alternative routes and methods of repatriating profits. The diversity of different connections allows the network to function even if some connections are broken—not least because the nodes and connections that remain intact can be redirected.

Although social networks exist independently of technological networks, there are major synergies among the two distinct network forms. The ability of transnational criminal networks to exploit the information and communication networks that developed during the 1990s provides major multiplier benefits. While exploitation of information technologies is certainly not the sole prerogative of network-based organisations, networks are extremely well placed to exploit new technological opportunities.

Indeed, many criminal organisations have been using technology as a force multiplier to carry out their entrepreneurial activities with greater efficiency at lower cost. There is one set of technologies in particular that could give them an enormous advantage in their continued competition with law enforcement—strong forms of encryption.

One of the most potent weapons of law enforcement in its struggle with organised crime has been the capacity to monitor communications among criminals—in effect, to identify and listen in on network connections. Encryption provides opportunities to neutralise this capacity and offers criminal networks a form of strategic superiority—the equivalent of an effective strategic defence initiative, at very low cost and based on off-the-shelf technologies. In sum, criminal networks provide moving and elusive targets that operate across enemy lines, infiltrating law enforcement agencies and governments, avoiding confrontation in favour of cooption and corruption.

In some networks, the tasks will be implicit and intuitive; in others, they are explicit and formal. In most criminal networks, the following roles are likely to be discernible:

i) *Organisers*: Those core individuals and groups that provide the steering mechanism for the network. These organisers will generally determine the scale and scope of activities and guidance and impetus for their execution.

iii) *Insulators*: Individuals or groups whose role is essentially to insulate the core from the danger posed by infiltration and compromise. These individuals transmit directives and guidance from the core to the periphery of the network. They also ensure that communication flows from the periphery do nothing to compromise the core.

iv) *Communicators*. Individuals who ensure that communication flows effectively from one node to another across the network as a whole. Their responsibility is to transmit directives from the core group and provide feedback. In some cases, insulators and communicators will be at odds because of competing impulses inherent in their differing responsibilities; in other cases the same individuals will combine both roles and make appropriate trade-offs.

v) *Guardians*: Enforcers concerned with the security of the network who take measures to minimise vulnerability to external attack or infiltration. Precautions about exactly who is recruited to the network combine with measures to ensure loyalty through a mix of ritual oaths and latent coercion directed against the new members or their families. Guardians act to prevent defections from the network, or in the event that such defections take place to ensure that the damage is minimised.

vi) *Extenders*: Those whose role is to extend the network by recruiting new members, by negotiating with other networks regarding collaboration, and by encouraging defectors from the world of business, government, and law enforcement. Where the extenders are successful, the network will have access to the portals of the licit world discussed above. Among the tactics that extenders typically use are voluntary recruitment through bribery and corruption and involuntary recruitment through coercion, sometimes leavened by the addition of rewards or inducements. Their targets typically include important and powerful politicians who can provide a high degree of protection, bureaucrats in particularly sensitive or pivotal positions, and financial managers who provide access to legitimate financial institutions.

vii) *Monitors*: Those who ensure the effectiveness of the network and whose responsibilities include reporting weaknesses and problems to the core organisers, who can then initiate remedial action. These network members are particularly crucial in ensuring implementation and providing guidance on appropriate corrective measures where necessary. They ensure that the network is able to adjust to new circumstances and maintain the high degree of flexibility that is critical to the capacity to circumvent law enforcement.

viii) *Crossovers*: People who have been recruited into a criminal network but who continue to operate in legal institutions, whether governmental, financial, or commercial.

Criminal networks are characterised by diversity in composition, density of connections, size, structure, shape, underlying bonding mechanisms, degree of sophistication, and scope of activities. Criminal networks engage in a variety of enterprises, the most lucrative of which is alien smuggling. Most criminal networks extend into the licit world for support. Some of the larger and more powerful criminal networks, however, take this process to considerable lengths and in effect create crossover figures who have very high-level positions in government.

One of the major problems in dealing with criminal networks is the absence of adequate models about precisely how these networks function. This is paralleled in the business world by a lack of understanding of why business networks succeed or fail. In neither domain has there been sufficient comparative work identifying patterns of success or failure. To overcome these problems it is essential to develop more effective intelligence about criminal networks. In this connection, various software companies, working closely with the law enforcement community, have developed some important tools to assist with the intelligence analysis task. Understanding network structures and operations makes it easier to identify vulnerabilities against which concentrated attacks should be directed.

Particularly important in this connection is the identification of critical nodes. A critical node in a network is one that generally has a high level of importance and a low level of redundancy. The importance can reflect the existence of certain specialised skills or the position of the node within the network. The low level of redundancy stems from the lack of adequate substitutes for those with these skills. In terms of network functions, a critical node might be a person who is well connected and the focus for dense connections.

Those nodes that are obviously critical, there are those that can become critical because of more general damage inflicted on the network. These nodes—the ones that are important but highly redundant–can become critical if they are attacked simultaneously or in close succession to one another. While this requires effective coordination, it is certainly an option that needs to be considered.

In attacking networks, it is also critical to target the boundaries, either from one network to another or from the criminal world to the upper world. Indeed, it is essential to disentangle the crime-corruption networks and thereby provide opportunities to detach the network from its various support structures. In part, the struggle between law enforcement and organised crime networks can be understood in terms of a competition in crossovers—informants and defectors from criminal networks on the one side and corrupted politicians, bureaucrats, law enforcement personnel, and members of the judiciary on the other.

One of the advantages criminal networks enjoy is that they are smart, future-oriented organisations locked in combat with governments that, by contrast, are often hobbled by a variety of constraints. Governments still operate along hierarchical lines and are further hindered by bureaucratic rivalry and competition, interagency antipathies, and a reluctance to share information and coordinate operations. Joint task forces, in which there are a pooling of resources and information and a concerted attack on a particular criminal network, provide an important value-added approach to attacking criminal networks. They can be particularly useful where they involve transnational cooperation in response to a transnational criminal network.

The idea of terrorists surreptitiously hacking into a computer system to introduce a virus, steal sensitive information, deface or swamp a website, or turn off a crucial public service seriously concerns computer security personnel around the world. High profile attacks—such as the denial-of-service (DOS) attacks against major e-commerce sites Yahoo! and e-Bay in 1999 or the ongoing 'cyber-jihad' against Israeli and American websites being waged by Pakistani-based hackers in support of the Palestinian 'al-Aqsa' Intifadah—continue to raise the spectre of cyber-terrorism. The Information Age is affecting not only the types of targets and weapons terrorists choose, but also the ways in which such groups operate and structure their organisations.

Several of the most dangerous terrorist organisations are using information technology (IT), such as computers, software, telecommunication devices, and the internet—to better organise and coordinate dispersed activities. Like the large numbers of private corporations that have embraced IT to operate more efficiently and with greater flexibility, terrorists are harnessing the power of IT to enable new operational doctrines and forms of organisation. And just as companies in the private sector are forming alliance networks to provide complex services to customers, so too are terrorist groups "desegregating" from hierarchical bureaucracies and moving to flatter, more decentralised, and often changing webs of groups united by a common goal.

The rise of networked arrangements in terrorist organisations is part of a wider move away from formally organised, state-sponsored groups to privately financed, loose networks of individuals and subgroups that may have strategic guidance but that, none the less, enjoy tactical independence. The new and more active generation of Middle Eastern groups has operated both inside and outside the region. For instance, in Israel and the occupied territories, Hamas and to a lesser extent the Palestinian Islamic Jihad have demonstrated their strength over the last five years with a series of suicide bombings that have killed more than 100 people. In Egypt, the Islamic Group (also known as al-Gama'a al-Islamiya) carried out a 1997 attack at Luxor, killing 58 tourists and four Egyptians. Another string of terrorist attacks (and foiled attempts) has focused attention on a loosely organised group of 'Arab Afghans'—radical Islamic fighters from several North African and Middle Eastern countries who have forged ties while resisting the Soviet occupation of Afghanistan.

These groups share the principles of the networked organisation—relative flatness, decentralisation and delegation of decisionmaking authority, and loose lateral ties among dispersed groups and individuals. The pro-Iranian Hizbollah in southern Lebanon acts as an umbrella organisation of radical Shiite groups and in many respects is a hybrid of hierarchical and network arrangements—although the organisational structure is formal, interactions among members are volatile and do not follow rigid lines of control. Perhaps the most interesting example of a terrorist netwar actor is Osama bin Laden's complex network of relatively autonomous groups that are financed from private sources.

Bin Laden uses his wealth and organisational skills to support and direct al Qaeda, a multinational alliance of Islamic extremists. Al Qaeda seeks to counter any perceived threats to Islam-wherever they come from—as indicated by bin Laden's 1996 declaration of a holy war against the United States and the West in general. In the declaration, he specified that such a holy war was to be waged by irregular, light, highly mobile forces. Although he finances al-Qaeda and directs some operations, he apparently does not play a direct command-and-control role over all operatives. Rather, he is a key figure in the coordination and support of several dispersed nodes.

Al Qaeda's command-and-control structure includes a consultation council ('majlis al shura'), which discusses and approves major undertakings, and possibly a military committee. At the heart of al Qaeda is bin Laden's inner core group, which sometimes conducts missions on its own. Most of the other member organisations remain independent, although the barriers between them are permeable.

Coordination mechanisms are enabled by advances in information technology—including increases in the speed of communication, reductions in the costs of communication, increases in bandwidth, vastly expanded connectivity, and the integration of communication and computing technologies. More specifically, new communication and computing technologies allow the establishment of networks in three critical ways. First, new technologies have greatly reduced transmission time, enabling dispersed organisational actors to communicate and coordinate their tasks. This phenomenon is not new—in the early twentieth century, the introduction of the telephone made it possible for large corporations to decentralise their operations through local branches.

Second, new technologies have significantly reduced the cost of communication, allowing information-intensive organisational designs such as networks to become viable. In the past, organisations sought to reduce coordination and communications costs by centralising and collocating those activities that are inherently more coordination-intensive. With the lowering of coordination costs, it is becoming increasingly possible to further desegregate organisations through decentralisation and autonomy.

Third, new technologies have substantially increased the scope and complexity of the information that can be shared, through the integration of computing with communications. Such innovations as tele- and computer-conferencing, groupware, internet chat, and websites allow participants to have "horizontal" and rich exchanges without requiring them to be located in close proximity. Thus, Information Age technologies are highly advantageous for a netwar group whose constituents are geographically dispersed or carry out distinct but complementary activities.

IT can be used to plan, coordinate, and execute operations. Using the internet for communication can increase the speed of mobilisation and allow more dialogue between members, which enhances the organisation's flexibility, since tactics can be adjusted more frequently. Individuals with a common agenda and goals can form subgroups, meet at a target location, conduct terrorist operations, and then readily terminate their relationships and redisperse.

The Laden network appears to have adopted information technology to support its networked mode of operations. Bin Laden allegedly uses satellite phone terminals to coordinate the activities of the group's dispersed operatives and has even devised counter-measures to ensure his safety while using such communication systems. Satellite phones reportedly travel in separate convoys from bin Laden's; the Saudi financier also refrains from direct use, often dictating his message to an assistant, who then relays it telephonically from a different location.

Bin Laden's operatives have used CD-ROM disks to store and disseminate information on recruiting, bomb making, heavy weapons, and terrorist operations. Egyptian computer experts who fought alongside bin Laden in the Afghan conflict are said to have helped him devise a communications network that relies on the web, e-mail, and electronic bulletin boards so that members can exchange information.

Counter-terrorist operations targeting Algerian Armed Islamic Group (GIA) bases in the 1990s uncovered computers and diskettes with instructions for the construction of bombs. In fact, it has been reported that the GIA makes heavy use of floppy disks and computers to store and process orders and other information for its members, who are dispersed in Algeria and Europe.

The militant Islamic group Hamas also uses the internet to share and communicate operational information. Hamas activists in the United States use chat rooms to plan operations and activities. Operatives use e-mail to coordinate actions across Gaza, the West Bank, and Lebanon. Hamas has realised that information can be passed relatively securely over the internet because counter-terrorism intelligence cannot accurately monitor the flow and content of all internet traffic. In fact, Israeli security officials cannot easily trace Hamas messages or decode their content.

Terrorist networks can protect their vital communication flows through readily available commercial technology, such as encryption programmes. New encryption programmes emerging on the commercial market are becoming so sophisticated that coded e-mails may soon be extremely difficult to break. In fact, strong encryption programmes are being integrated into commercial applications and network protocols so that soon encryption will be easy and automatic.

Terrorists can also use steganography—a method of hiding secret data in other data such as embedding a secret message within a picture file. Terrorists can also encrypt cell phone transmissions, steal cell phone numbers and programme them into a single phone, or use prepaid cell phone cards purchased anonymously to keep their communications secure. The latest communications technologies are thus enabling terrorists to operate from almost any country in the world, provided they have access to the necessary IT infrastructure; and this affects the ways in which groups rely on different forms of sponsorship. The networked terrorists may have a reduced need for state support-indeed, governmental protection may become less necessary if technologies such as encryption allow a terrorist group to operate with a greater degree of stealth and safety.

For the foreseeable future, electronically mediated coordination will not be able to entirely supplant face-to-face exchanges, because uncertainty and risk will continue to characterise most organisational choices and interactions among individuals. Moreover, informal linkages and the shared values mentioned above—which are critical enablers of networked designs—can only be fostered through personal contact.

Electronically mediated exchange can increase the range, amount, and velocity of information flow in a network organisation. But the viability and effectiveness of this electronic network will depend critically on an underlying network of social relationships based on face-to-face interaction. Moreover, while IT-enabled communication flows can greatly help a network coordinate dispersed activities, they can also present a security risk.

Communications over electronic channels can become a liability, since it leaves digital "traces". There are some examples of how electronic information belonging to terrorist groups has fallen into the hands of law enforcement personnel. In 1995, Hamas's Abd-al-Rahman Zaydan was arrested and his computer seized—the computer contained a database of Hamas contact information that was used to apprehend other suspects. In December 1999, 15 terrorists linked to Osama bin Laden were arrested in Jordan; along with bomb-making materials, rifles, and radio-controlled detonators, a number of computer disks were seized. Intelligence analysts were able to extract information about bomb building and terrorist training camps in Afghanistan. In June 2000, the names of 19 suspects were found on computer disks recovered from a Hizbollah-controlled house. This makes it likely that terrorist groups will adopt designs that fall short of fully connected, all-channel networks. Hybrids of hierarchies and networks may better reflect the relative costs and benefits of greater IT reliance—as well as further the group's mission.

IT can also improve terrorist intelligence collection and analysis, as well as offensive information operations (IO). The acquisition by terrorist groups of an offensive IO capability could represent a significant threat as the world becomes more dependent on information and communications flows. The Information Age technology can help terrorists conduct three broad types of offensive IO. First, it can aid them in their perception management and propaganda activities. Next, such technology can be used to attack virtual targets for disruptive purposes. Finally, IT can be used to cause physical destruction. Given the importance of knowledge and soft power to the conduct of netwar, it is not surprising that networked terrorists have already begun to leverage IT for perception management and propaganda to influence public opinion, recruit new members, and generate funding.

Getting a message out and receiving extensive news media exposure are important components of terrorist strategy, which ultimately seeks to undermine the will of an opponent. In addition to such traditional media as television or print, the internet now offers terrorist groups an alternative way to reach out to the public, often with much more direct control over their message. The news media play an integral part in a terrorist act because they are the conduit for news of the violence to the general population.

Terrorists have improved their media management techniques to the point of using "spin doctoring" tactics. In fact, some groups have even acquired their own television and radio stations to take direct control of the reporting of events. Hizbollah, through its television station, has broadcast footage of strikes carried out by its operatives and has a sophisticated media centre that regularly—and professionally—briefs foreign journalists. Hizbollah field units have even included specially designated cameramen to record dramatic video footage of Israeli casualties that was then aired in Lebanon and usually rebroadcast by Israeli television.

Before the internet, a bombing might be accompanied by a phone call or fax to the press by a terrorist claiming responsibility. Now, bombings can be followed—should terrorists so desire—by an immediate press release from their own websites. The fact that many terrorists now have direct control over the content of their message offers further opportunities for perception management, as well as for image manipulation, special effects, and deception.

An internet presence could prove advantageous for mobilising "part-time cyberterrorists"—individuals not directly affiliated with a given terrorist group who none the less support its agenda and who use malicious software tools and instructions available at a terrorist website. This scenario would closely resemble the initiatives taken by both the Israeli and Palestinian governments, which have encouraged private citizens to download computer attack tools and become involved in the conflict surrounding the al-Aqsa Intifadah. It appears that nearly all terrorist groups have a web presence. As the table indicates, Hizbollah even manages multiple sites, each with a different purpose. Websites can also be used to refine or customise recruiting techniques.

Using some of the same marketing techniques employed by commercial enterprises, terrorist servers could capture information about the users who browse their websites, and then later contact those who seem most interested. Recruiters may also use more interactive internet technology to roam online chat rooms and cyber cafes looking for receptive members of the public, particularly young people.

Electronic bulletin boards and user nets can also serve as vehicles for reaching out to potential recruits. Interested computer users around the world can be engaged in long-term "cyber relationships" that could lead to friendship and eventual membership. Netwar-oriented terrorists can also use IT to launch disruptive attacks, that is, electronic strikes that temporarily disable, but do not destroy, physical and/or virtual infrastructure. If the ultimate goal of a terrorist is to influence his opponent's will to fight, IO offer additional means to exert influence beyond using simple physical attacks to cause terror.

Disruptive attacks include "choking" computer systems through such tools as e-bombs, fax spamming, and hacking techniques to deface websites. These strikes are usually non-lethal in nature, although they can wreak havoc and cause significant economic damage. To date, disruptive strikes by terrorists have been relatively few and fairly unsophisticated, but they do seem to be increasing in frequency. For example, in 1996, the Liberation Tigers of Tamil Eelam (LTTE) launched an e-mail bomb attack against Sri Lankan diplomatic missions. Using automated tools, the guerilla organisation flooded Sri Lankan embassies with thousands of messages, thus establishing a "virtual blockade". In 2000, a group of Pakistani hackers who call themselves the Muslim Online Syndicate (MOS) defaced more than 500 websites in India to protest the conflict in Kashmir. Finally, Pakistan's Lashkar-e-Taiba claimed to have attacked Indian military websites in early 2000. Disruptive rather than destructive actions take place for several reasons.

For example, terrorists who rely on the internet for perception management and communication purposes may prefer not to take "the net" down, but rather to slow it down selectively. In addition, groups may want to rely on non-lethal cyber strikes to pressure governments without alienating their own constituent audiences. Terrorist groups may also follow the lead of criminal hackers and use the threat of disruptive attacks to blackmail and extort funds from private-sector entities.

IT-driven information operations can lead to the actual destruction of physical or virtual systems. Malicious viruses and worms can be used to permanently destroy or corrupt data and cause economic damage. In the worst case, these same software tools can be used to cause destructive failure in a critical infrastructure like air traffic control, power, or water systems, which can lead to casualties. Indeed, it is likely that information operations that result in the loss of life may offer the same level of drama as physical attacks with bombs. Also, striking targets through electronic means does not carry the risks associated with using conventional weapons—such as handling explosives or being in close proximity to the target.

The lack of destructive information attacks is arguably influenced by the relative difficulty of electronically destroying critical infrastructure components—the level of protection of existing infrastructure may be too high for terrorists to overcome with their current IT skill set. In fact, a terrorist organisation would first have to overcome significant technical hurdles to develop an electronic attack capability. Concentrating the necessary technical expertise and equipment to damage or destroy targeted information systems is no easy task, given the computer security risks involved. In developing and increasing their reliance on electronic attacks, terrorist organisations may be assuming risks and costs associated with the relative novelty of the technology.

Terrorists wishing to expand the scope of their offensive IO activities would have to continue upgrading and researching new technologies to keep up with the counter-measures available to computer security experts and systems administrators. This technology "treadmill" would demand constant attention and the diversion of scarce organisational resources. Another important determinant in netwar terrorists choosing low-level IT is that such conventional weapons as bombs remain more cost-effective.

In fact, most terrorism experts believe that existing groups see their current tactics as sufficient and are not interested in branching into computer network attacks. Since current tactics are simple and successful, there is no built-in demand to innovate: bombing still works. As long as current tactics enable these groups to accomplish their short-term goals and move toward their long-term goals, there will be no strong incentives to change behaviour. Disruptive attacks may be easier to carry out, but because of their very nature they do not produce the same kind of visceral and emotional reaction that the loss of human life does.

FEATURES OF CYBER-TERRORISM

Cyber-terrorism is the unlawful attacks and threats of attack against computers, networks, and the information stored therein when done to intimidate or coerce a government or its people in furtherance of political or social objectives. Further, to qualify as cyber-terrorism, an attack should result in violence against persons or property, or at least cause enough harm to generate fear. Attacks that lead to death or bodily injury, explosions, plane crashes, water contamination, or severe economic loss would be examples.

Serious attacks against critical infrastructures could be acts of cyber-terrorism, depending on their impact. Attacks that disrupt non-essential services or that are mainly a costly nuisance would not. Cyberspace is constantly under assault. Cyber spies, thieves, saboteurs, and thrill seekers break into computer systems, steal personal data and trade secrets, vandalise Websites, disrupt service, sabotage data and systems, launch computer viruses and worms, conduct fraudulent transactions, and harass individuals and companies.

These attacks are facilitated with increasingly powerful and easy-to-use software tools, which are readily available for free from thousands of Websites on the internet. Many of the attacks are serious and costly. The recent I LOVE YOU virus and variants, for example, was estimated to have hit tens of millions of users and cost billions of dollars in damage. Some attacks are conducted in furtherance of political and social objectives.

These attacks were motivated by political and social reasons, whether they were sufficiently harmful or frightening to be classified as cyber-terrorism is a judgement call. To understand the potential threat of cyber-terrorism, two factors must be considered:

i) whether there are targets that are vulnerable to attack that could lead to violence or severe harm, and
ii) whether there are actors with the capability and motivation to carry them out.

Even if the technology itself offers good security, it is frequently configured or used in ways that make it open to attack. While many hackers have the knowledge, skills, and tools to attack computer systems, they generally lack the motivation to cause violence or severe economic or social harm. Conversely, terrorists who are motivated to cause violence seem to lack the capability or motivation to cause that degree of damage in cyberspace. Terrorists do use cyberspace to facilitate traditional forms of terrorism such as bombings. They put up Websites to spread their messages and recruit supporters, and they use the internet to communicate and coordinate action.

Both the revolutionary and ethno-nationalist separatists are likely to seek an advanced-structured capability. The far-right extremists are likely to settle for a simple-unstructured capability, as cyber-terror offers neither the intimacy nor cathartic effects that are central to the psychology of far-right terror. Thus, at this time, cyber-terrorism does not seem to pose an imminent threat. For a terrorist, it would have some advantages over physical methods. Indeed cyber-terrorism could be immensely appealing precisely because of the tremendous attention given to it by the government and media.

Cyber-terrorism has some drawbacks. Systems are complex, so it may be harder to control an attack and achieve a desired level of damage than using physical weapons. Unless people are injured, there is also less drama and emotional appeal. Further, terrorists may be disinclined to try new methods unless they see their old ones as inadequate, particularly when the new methods require considerable knowledge and skill to use effectively. Terrorists generally stick with tired and true methods.

Novelty and sophistication of attack may be much less important than assurance that a mission will be operationally successful. Indeed, the risk of operational failure could be a deterrent to terrorists. For now, the truck bomb poses a much greater threat than the logic bomb. The next generation of terrorists will grow up in a digital world, with ever more powerful and easy-to-use hacking tools at their disposal. They might see greater potential for cyber-terrorism than the terrorists of today, and their level of knowledge and skill relating to hacking will be greater.

Cyber-terrorism could also become more attractive as the real and virtual worlds become more closely coupled, with a greater number of physical devices attached to the internet. Some of these may be remotely controlled. Terrorists, for example, might target robots used in tele-surgery.

NETWAR STRATEGIES

The term netwar refers to an emerging mode of conflict at societal levels, short of traditional military warfare, in which the protagonists use network forms of organisation and related doctrines, strategies, and technologies attuned to the Information Age. These protagonists are likely to consist of dispersed organisations, small groups, and individuals who communicate, coordinate, and conduct their campaigns in an internetted manner, often without a precise central command. Thus, netwar differs from modes of conflict and crime in which the protagonists prefer to develop formal, stand-alone, hierarchical organisations, doctrines, and strategies as in past efforts.

The term netwar is meant to call attention to the prospect that network-based conflict and crime will become major phenomena in the decades ahead. Various actors across the spectrum of conflict and crime are already evolving in this direction. This includes familiar adversaries who are modifying their structures and strategies to take advantage of networked designs, e.g., transnational terrorist groups, blackmarket proliferators of weapons of mass destruction (WMD), drug and other crime syndicates, fundamentalist and ethno-nationalist movements, intellectual-property pirates, and immigration and refugee smugglers.

Today's terrorists, characterised by religious and social motivations, stand at the threshold of netwar. The lighting rods of post-modern conflict, these terrorists eschew terrorism's classic political motivations and instead seek broader religious or social change. This resurgence of religious terrorism involves Shi'a and Sunni Islamists seeking to replace the secular state, such Christian fundamentalists as the Army of God in the United States, the racist Christian Identity movement, and some fundamentalist Jews in Israel.

Millenarian cults have also sprung up, perhaps best exemplified by the Aum Shinrikyo's international conspiracy to wield weapons of mass destruction, which culminated in a campaign of chemical and biological assaults, including the sarin attack on the Tokyo subway. Aum continues to exist and is once again building membership under the name Aleph. These post-modern religious zealots rely in large measure on common philosophy rather than rigid individual command and control to reach their ends.

Bin Laden not only provided philosophical guidance to his own network (al Qaeda), but was able to bring together an amalgam of separate but like-minded groups, including Gama's al-Islamiya (Egypt), the Ulema Society and Harkat-ul-Ansar (Pakistan), and the Jihad Movement (Bangladesh), into a networked alliance. This alliance, sharing the goals of the Islamic Army for the Liberation of the Holy Places, was able to come together to conduct specific operations in the near-simultaneous bombing of the US embassies in Kenya and Tanzania.

Some urban gangs, back-country militias, and militant single-issue groups in the United States have also been developing netwar-like attributes. The netwar spectrum also includes a new generation of revolutionaries, radicals, and activists who are beginning to create Information Age ideologies, in which identities and loyalties may shift from the nation state to the transnational level of "global civil society".

New kinds of actors, such as anarchistic and nihilistic leagues of computer-hacking "cyboteurs", may also engage in netwar. Many—if not most—netwar actors will be non-state, even stateless. Some may be agents of a state, but others may try to turn states into their agents. Also, a netwar actor may be both subnational and transnational in scope. The full spectrum of netwar proponents may thus seem broad and odd at first glance. But there is an underlying pattern that cuts across all variations: the use of network forms of organisation, doctrine, strategy, and technology attuned to the Information Age.

Netwar is a result of the rise of network forms of organisation, which in turn is partly a result of the computerised information revolution. To realise its potential, a fully interconnected network requires a capacity for constant, dense information and communications flows, more so than do other forms of organisation. This capacity is afforded by the latest information and communication technologies—cellular telephones, fax machines, electronic mail, websites, and computer conferencing. Such technologies are highly advantageous for netwar actors whose constituents are geographically dispersed.

On the offence, networks tend to be adaptable, flexible, and versatile *vis-a-vis* opportunities and challenges. This may be particularly the case where a set of actors can engage in swarming. Little analytic attention has been given to swarming, which is quite different from traditional mass—and manoeuvre-oriented approaches to conflict. Yet swarming may become the key mode of conflict in the Information Age, and the cutting edge for this possibility is found among netwar protagonists. Swarming is a seemingly amorphous, but deliberately structured, coordinated, strategic way to strike from all directions at a particular point or points, by means of a sustainable pulsing of force and/or fire, close-in as well as from standoff positions. This notion of "force and/ or fire" may be literal in the case of military or police operations, but metaphorical in the case of NGO activists, who may, for example, be blocking city intersections or emitting volleys of e-mails and faxes.

Swarming will work best—perhaps it will only work—if it is designed mainly around the deployment of myriad, small, dispersed, networked manoeuvre units. Swarming occurs when the dispersed units of a network of small forces converge on a target from multiple directions. The overall aim is sustainable pulsing—swarm networks must be able to coalesce rapidly and stealthily on a target, then dissever and redisperse, immediately ready to re-combine for a new pulse. The capacity for a "stealthy approach" suggests that, in netwar, attacks are more likely to occur in "swarms" than in more traditional "waves". Swarming may be most effective, and difficult to defend against, where a set of netwar actors do not "mass" their forces, but rather engage in dispersion and "packetisation".

The blurring of offence and defence reflects another feature of netwar. It tends to defy and cut across standard boundaries, jurisdictions, and distinctions between state and society, public and private, war and peace, war and crime, civilian and military, police and military, and legal and illegal. This makes it difficult if not impossible for a government to assign responsibility to any single agency, e.g., military, police, or intelligence, to be in charge of responding.

A netwar actor may aim to confound people's fundamental beliefs about the nature of their culture, society, and government, partly to foment fear but perhaps mainly to disorient people and unhinge their perceptions. This is why a netwar with a strong social content—whether waged by ethno-nationalists, terrorists, or social activists—may tend to be about disruption more than destruction. The more epistemological the challenge, the more confounding it may be from an organisational standpoint.

In netwar, things are rarely so clear. A protagonist is likely to operate in the cracks and gray areas of a society, striking where lines of authority crisscross and the operational paradigms of politicians, officials, soldiers, police officers, and related actors get fuzzy and clash.

Moreover, where transnational participation is strong, a netwar's protagonists may expose a local government to challenges to its sovereignty and legitimacy by arousing foreign governments and business corporations to put pressure on the local government to alter its domestic policies and practices.

Netwar is a deduced concept—it derives from our thinking about the effects and implications of the information revolution. Once coined, the concept helps show that evidence is mounting about the rise of network forms of organisation, and about the importance of "information strategies" and "information operations" across the spectrum of conflict, including among ethnonationalists, terrorists, guerrillas, criminals, and activists. Netwar can be waged by "good" as well as "bad" actors, and through peaceful as well as violent measures. From its beginnings, netwar has appealed to a broad cross-section of non-state actors who are striving to confront or cope with their state authorities.

Ethno-nationalists, criminals, and terrorists—all have found new power in networking. But so too have emerging global civil society actors who have emphasised non-violent efforts to win the 'battle of the story'—a more purely informational dimension of netwar—rather than the violent swarming characteristic of its darker side. Both categories of actors seem to realise, even if only implicitly, that, in the future, conflict will become even more 'irregularised', with the set-piece confrontations and battles of earlier eras largely disappearing.

The duality of netwar in the real world—dark-side criminals and terrorists on the one hand, but enlightening civil society forces on the other–is mirrored in the virtual world of cyberspace, which is increasingly utilised for crime and terror, along with social activism. At present, social activism is far more robust and established in the cyber realm than is crime or terror.

In netwar, alliances between and among state and non-state actors can fuel conflict. Combinations of "internetted" transnational criminal organisations (TCOs), triads, cartels, cults, terrorists, gangs, and other entities replace their more state-oriented predecessors. Gangs operating in urban areas have gone through three generational changes—from traditional turf gangs, to market-oriented drug gangs, to a new generation that may mix political and mercenary elements.

Particularly important for this evolution are trends in the degree of politicisation, internationalisation, and sophistication of a gang. Politicisation refers to the scope of political activity embraced by the gang. Internationalisation refers to the spatial or geographic reach of the gang. Most gangs are extremely local in nature, generally spanning several blocks of turf. Traditional street gangs operate at the low end of extreme societal violence. Primarily turf-oriented, they are characterised by loose leadership with a focus on loyalty and turf protection in their immediate neighbourhoods. Members of such gangs engage in opportunistic criminal activity, including rivalry for drug sales as lone individuals and as a gang competing with other gangs.

Like some militant net-activists, violent networked groups benefit from the obscurity and near simultaneous transmission of information inherent in new network-enhancing technology. It appears that contact with other sophisticated networked groups may help to "revolutionise" groups at the lower stages of progress, enabling them to become full-fledged criminal and terrorist netwar actors. As these groups become more sophisticated and obtain more skills and technology through the vast amount of illicit funds at their disposal, it may only be a matter of time until they learn to attack cyber as well as physical infrastructures, and to use information warfare to their advantage. Groups with a natural network structure are able to quickly learn to exploit new technologies and organisational ideas to make the group more successful.

Police, military, and security forces must learn to integrate network forms into their hierarchical structures to enable rapid, robust, and flexible response across organisational and political boundaries. Otherwise, networked adversaries may exploit the gaps and seams between governmental organisations. These must be filled through innovative, multilateral, inter-agency collaboration. An important strategic intelligence task for police and law enforcement agencies combating these groups is identification of evidence of the diffusion of information technologies and/or networked forms among urban gangs, hooligans, and violent anarchist cells.

Netwar, because of its dependence on networks, is facilitated by the radical increases in global and transnational connectivity, as well as from the growing opportunities for increased connectivity in another sense—the ability of "outsiders" and "insiders" to gain access to each other, and even for insiders to be secreted within an organisation or sector of society. Netwar rests on the dynamics of networks.

In netwar, leadership remains important, even though the protagonists may make every effort to have a leaderless design. One way to accomplish this is to have many leaders diffused throughout the network who try to act in coordination, without central control or a hierarchy. This can create coordination problems—a typical weakness of network designs—but, as often noted, it can also obviate counter-leadership targeting. Perhaps a more significant, less noted point is that the kind of leader who may be most important for the development and conduct of a netwar is not the "great man" or the administrative leadership that people are accustomed to seeing, but rather the doctrinal leadership—the individual or set of individuals who, far from acting as commander, is in charge of shaping the flow of communications, the "story" expressing the netwar, and the doctrine guiding its strategy and tactics.

In netwars, swarming often appears not only in real-life actions but also through measures in cyberspace. Aspirations for a leaderless swarming doctrine, beginning with a rationale and a capability for "electronic civil disobedience", show up among hacktivists who advocate the usage of online tools to flood a target's computer systems, e-mail inboxes, and websites, thereby disrupting and even defacing them.

Current advances in peer-to-peer computing may give netwar actors an even greater technological edge in the future. Netwar can be waged without necessarily having access to the internet and other advanced technologies. This level may mix old and new, low- and high-tech capabilities. Human couriers and face-to-face meetings may still remain essential, especially for secretive actors like terrorists and criminals.

Netwar works, and it is working for all types: good guys and bad guys, civil and uncivil actors. So far, all have done quite well, generally, in their various confrontations with nation states. International criminal networks, including traditional organised crime groups and drug-trafficking organisations, have taken advantage of the dramatic changes in technology, world politics, and the global economy to become more sophisticated and flexible in their operations. They have extensive worldwide networks and infrastructure to support their criminal operations. Much more than in the past, criminal organisations are networking and cooperating with one another, enabling them to merge expertise and to broaden the scope of their activities.

The modern-day netwar equivalent corresponds to the dark-side terrorists, criminals, and ethnonationalists who pursue self-assertion for narrow purposes. In other words, netwar is not a uniformly adverse phenomenon that can, or should, always be countered. The rise of netwar and its many early successes imply the need for statecraft to adjust to—perhaps be transformed by—these civil and uncivil manifestations of the information revolution. Most central concepts about national security are over half a century old now. Containment, mutual deterrence, coercive diplomacy, all seem ever less relevant to the types of challenges confronting nation states. Netwar—with its emphasis on empowering dispersed small groups, its reliance on the power of the story, and its suitability to leaderless networks adept at swarming—should call forth a strategic renaissance among those who would either employ it or oppose it.

While traditional street gang activity does not constitute terrorism in the classic sense, it acts as a conflict generator that may provide the necessary foundation for some groups to evolve into complex internetted criminal entities, or even net-warriors. Such street gangs, while violent, have been viewed as outside of the realm of true terrorism because of their lack of formal organisation. Yet informal, network-like organisation is one of the factors that may make netwar more difficult to combat than classic terrorism.

While street gangs may be in a position to exploit changes in social organisation, the majority of street gangs remain firmly in the first or second generation. These gangs tactically employ limited quasi-terrorism to support their activities. Like other organised crime groups, such street gangs use criminal terror, targeting each other, or interfering agencies, to sustain spatial or economic spheres of influence—'turf' or 'markets'.

Some gangs are becoming increasingly mobile, gaining in sophistication, developing links with organised crime entities, and maintaining caches of weapons financed by the large sums of money obtained from multi-state or cross-border narcotics distribution networks. An interesting variation on the traditional turf gang is the rise of soccer hooligans in Europe; for them, the important turf is not a neighbourhood *per se*, but more a 'virtual turf', as represented by their favourite local or national soccer team.

Hooligans are integrating network and hierarchical command and control to enhance their combat effectiveness with technology. Firms of opposing hooligans now use wireless technology and the internet for both marshalling their own combatants and challenging their opponents.

In the future, netwar actors will continue to consolidate their IT use primarily for organisational purposes, with some emphasis on perception management on the offensive IO side. Under these conditions, networked terrorists would still rely on such traditional weapons as conventional bombs to cause physical violence. But they will also transmit information on how to build such weapons via CD-ROMs or e-mail, use chat rooms to coordinate their activities, and use websites to publicise and justify their strikes to a global audience.

New groups could even be led by individuals who are technically skilled, suggesting the rise of a hybrid breed of "terrorists-cum-hackers". Like hackers, they would undertake most of their attacks in cyberspace. Like terrorists, they would seek to strike targets by both disruptive and destructive means to further a political or religious agenda. The acquisition and use of Information Age technology by terrorist groups are far from certain. Some terrorist networks may even become sophisticated enough to sustain and coordinate offensive campaigns in both the virtual and physical realms. What is certain, however, is that counter-terrorism policy will be able to counter the dangers associated with terrorist IT use only if it becomes attuned to the Information Age. Counter-terrorist policies and tactics could even alter the speed with which terrorists become informatised—groups facing a robust counter-terrorism campaign may have less time and resources to acquire new technologies.

REFERENCES

Denning, P. J., *Computers Under Attack: Intruders, Worms, and Viruses*, Addison-Wesley, 1990.

FBIS, "Arab Afghans Said to Launch Worldwide Terrorist War", *Paris al-Watan al-'Arabi*, December 1, pp. 22–24, 1995.

Hoffman, Bruce, "Responding to Terrorism Across the Technological Spectrum", in John Arquilla and David Ronfeldt, eds., *In Athena's Camp: Preparing for Conflict in the Information Age*, Santa Monica, Calif.: RAND, pp. 339–367, 1997.

Kurlantzick, Joshua, "Muslim Separatists in Global Network of Terrorist Groups", *Washington Times*, May 2, 2000.

Nacos, Brigitte, *Terrorism and the Media,* New York: Columbia University Press, 1994.

______________ Nohria, Nitin, and Robert Eccles, eds., *Networks and Organizations*, Boston, Mass.: Harvard Business School Press, 1992.

Whine, Michael, "Islamist Organizations on the Internet," *Terrorism and Political Violence*, Vol. 11, No. 1, Spring 1999.

Williams, Phil, "Transnational Criminal Organisations and International Security", *Survival*, Vol. 36, No. 1, pp. 96–113, 1994.

4

Deterrence and Prevention

The current revolution in computing, telecommunications, and information technologies is profoundly remaking our society, our democracy, and our daily lives. From a military perspective, visionaries within the military forces see in the new technologies of the information revolution the means to radically increase military effectiveness, reduce casualties, and save money.

If that society undergoes a change as profound as the information revolution, its security requirements will change as well. The most important consequence of the information revolution for the military forces will not be the application of new information technologies to its existing missions, as the military perspective often implies. Rather, the most important effect will be the need for the military forces to adapt itself to performing new and different missions.

Since the release of nuclear energy, no technological development has so preoccupied the military forces as the currently cresting revolution in computing, telecommunications, and information technologies. Some see the information revolution as but one component of an ongoing revolution in military affairs, in which the information technologies, when combined with new concepts for military operations and their command and control, will usher in a revolution in warfare comparable to that which occurred with blitzkrieg and aircraft carriers in World War II.

MILITARY-TECHNICAL REVOLUTION (MTR)

Exploitation of information technologies necessitate major changes in the ways militaries think about, organise themselves for, and wage combat now. The ongoing Information Revolution is having equally important, if less obvious effects on the post-Cold War security environment. There is, for example, a broad agreement in the defence community that the 1991 Gulf War marked the early stages of a "Military Technical Revolution" (MTR) which promises to transform the character of war as radically as did the advent of nuclear weapons 50 years age. Driving this revolution are advances in surveillance, communications, and information-processing technologies, which create the possibility of imbuing the "information loop of warfare" with unprecedented accuracy and speed, thereby achieving "information dominance" over less capable adversaries now.

Information technology is said to herald revolutionary changes in everything from the sources of economic wealth to the very nature of combat. As all of this diverse activity implies, the world is clearly changing in dramatic ways. However, not all changes are revolutions. For the word revolution to have meaning, at least in a defence policy sense, it must imply a degree of change that requires radical adaptations in current modes of strategies, doctrines, and forms of organisation. Current strategies, doctrines, and organisations can incorporate the current changes with only evolutionary adaptations.

History offers few examples of contemporary observers who correctly assessed an ongoing revolution, but many examples of false prophets. However, because such revolutions offer tremendous rewards to nations that can accurately anticipate them and tremendous costs to those that miss the wave of the future, the pressure to catch the wave can prove irresistible. This pressure reflects the many historical instances of disasters befalling nations and groups that have failed to adapt themselves effectively to new technological possibilities. The catastrophic defeat of the French Army in 1940, for example, is typically attributed to its leaders' failure to fully comprehend the revolutionary implications of the new technologies of tanks, airplanes, and radios for the modern battlefields.

No nation or military can afford the disruptions and upheavals caused by excessively frequent reorganisations. False revolutions also impose a severe cost in terms of wasted effort, chaotic disruption of routine, and inappropriate innovations. In Britain, during the inter-war period, for example, the idea that strategic bombing had revolutionised warfare helped promote the idea that a large land army and fighter aircraft were unnecessary, so Britain channelled scarce resources into a heavy bomber fleet, with nearly disastrous consequences. Complete reorganisations, in particular, impose large costs and should not be made prematurely.

The creation of a corps of information warriors today, as some people advocate, might make as much sense as a corps of internal combustion warriors would have at the beginning of the twentieth century. Inappropriate or even premature adaptations can be as wasteful and as detrimental to effectiveness as a failure to innovate. This potential for 'over-innovation' explains why the use of the word revolution has important policy implications. Evolutionary change implies the type of almost reflexive adaptation and flexibility that, however difficult, militaries can and should do most every day. Revolutions, in contrast, are infrequent cataclysmic events that require revisiting all the old assumptions that pass unnoticed in daily life.

Declaring a revolution opens the field to proposals for wholesale transformations in doctrine, equipment, and even personnel. Indeed, such transformations are a necessary condition of a revolution in military affairs. For this reason, historians seeking to categorise past innovations as revolutionary often look for major, permanent changes in organisational structure as an indication of revolution. If evolutionary adaptation of the type seen continually in large organisations could meet the requirements of a revolution, the word revolution would have no practical meaning.

Similarly, revolutionary changes typically need to be identified and responded to by those outside the mainstream of the organisation in question. Insiders concerned with the day-to-day strains of getting the job done often lose sight of the big picture or become so accustomed, even attached emotionally or professionally, to the current modes of operation that they refuse to contemplate dramatic change.

If revolutionary advances in information technology have rendered that experience less relevant to the changes needed to adapt to new technology, outsiders' views will be given greater weight. Use of the word revolution, therefore, implies greater scope and necessity for outsiders to delve into the internal workings of military organisations and recommend or even force changes against entrenched cultures that have become dangerously outmoded.

Military professionals who choose to use the word revolution to characterise the current changes in warfare need to understand that they are inviting, even impelling, civilian intervention in issues usually left to the military. Military revolution sees information technology as providing new means to an old end: victory in conflicts between traditional military organisations. This application of information technology to the problem of warfare does not claim to redefine the meaning of victory or to change the actors involved in any essential way. Rather, it promises to improve dramatically the capability of militaries to apply combat power. In this way, the "information-based revolution in military affairs" appears as only the latest in a series of technological or social changes that have profoundly remade warfare.

Such a revolution has a tendency to create sudden, dramatic changes in the relative combat power of military organisations. In current writing on the military revolution, the key technologies that are transforming warfare are usually identified as information technologies—although how specifically such technologies will affect military affairs is an issue of great dispute. For many, the idea of a global or national information infrastructure has created a new medium for battle: "cyberspace," akin to air, land, sea, or space. In a conscious analogy to air warfare, this type of information warfare often involves securing information superiority or "information dominance" in the new medium. Information dominance means that your side has the ability to collect, communicate, and protect information without disruption, while the other side does not. It enables the possessor to seize air dominance easily and, from there, to move on to relatively unimpeded land operations. This implies that the new dependence of society and the military on information systems has made information the new centre of gravity, the central, most critical node in any nation's ability to wage war.

In strategic information warfare, the battleground is the information infrastructure upon which modern societies have become so dependent, including the electric power grid, the financial system, the air traffic control system, and a variety of sensitive computer systems. It draws its inspiration from the internet and makes widespread use of the internet metaphor. The interconnectivity of these systems renders them vulnerable to systemic disruptions. The ability to access these systems from abroad makes them susceptible to attacks whose origin is difficult to identify. Indeed, done with enough subtlety and skill, it might, according to some accounts, become difficult even to know one is under attack until it is too late.

Although the information infrastructure that strategic information-warfare theorists worry about encompasses much more than just the internet, that network is so closely associated with this infrastructure that, for many, they are essentially equivalent terms. As a result, the dangers and pitfalls of the internet, outlined above, form the basis for most of the hypothesised threats to the information infrastructure. Frequent reports of computer accidents, computer crime, and possible "infoterrorism" have fixed in the public mind that remote access capability, the lack of central control, and interconnectivity mean that the internet and computers in general are irremediably insecure. Many of these reports are sensationalist or simply wrong, but a lack of general technical understanding of how computers and modern networks work has created an environment ripe for rumour and speculation.

Although strategic information warfare is clearly a possibility, the popular success of the internet and the consequent extension of the internet metaphor to the information infrastructure as a whole has caused the threat to be blown out of proportion. The internet is a system with an open architecture specifically designed to facilitate exchange of information and easy access, with little attention, as yet, given to problems of security. Its decentralised, explosive growth, its large public profile, and its ethic of free exchange have reinforced these security problems.

The operational level of information warfare involves exploiting the battlefield applications of new information technologies to create a system of systems. This system would give the commander nearly complete knowledge of the battlefield. It consists of a suite of full-time sensors, data fusers, and interpreters in combination with instantaneous command, control, and communication systems; precise navigation; and electronic warfare, among others, which together create a "synergistic" increase in combat power that constitutes an information-based revolution in military affairs. A critical element of this concept is the ability to use the information that the system of systems has gathered, processed, and disseminated.

Thus, beyond information technologies, this revolution is enabled by the introduction and spread of precision-guided weaponry that can exploit the new information and serve as the blunt edge of the system of systems. None the less, for these theorists, this is an information-based revolution because, with the eventual widespread availability of precision-guided weapons, the ability to achieve efficient information processes becomes the key element of skill that differentiates military organisations.

Information systems for command, control, and communication become so essential to combat operations that warfare becomes, conceptually, a contest between these systems rather than between strike systems, with information systems themselves as the most critical targets. In stark contrast to strategic information warfare, the operational level of information warfare distinctly favours an American military establishment that is further along and better positioned to take advantage of military applications of information technology.

Historians typically take a long view and see a military revolution as an observable breaking point between two recognisably different types of warfare. War mostly meant fighting on open plains between massed armies, since fortresses were virtually useless in the face of artillery. This view of military revolutions tends to downplay the role of human agency in the making of a revolution. Such revolutions stem from exogenous forces, which were bound, sooner or later, to spark a fundamental shift in the methods of war. Technological, demographic, or social changes in this sense "push" the revolution into being.

Although the intellectual spark that reveals the possibility of a revolution gives a temporary, and possibly large, advantage to one side, that advantage is usually short-lived as the new method of fighting is copied by one's rivals. After this period of emulation, the main thing that has changed is warfare itself. Any lasting effect on the relative power of states depends less on the intervening events than on the inherent geographical, social, or cultural advantages that particular states possess in adopting the revolution.

The currently proposed information-based revolution in military affairs has been the most self-conscious military revolution in history, yet most commentators have largely passed over the question of whether they see themselves as creating a strategist's revolution or predicting an historian's. While both types of revolution have analytical validity in retrospect, the utility of the historian's viewpoint to inform the current debate is very limited. While contemporaries can and must create military revolutions in the strategic sense, their ability to predict military revolutions in the historic sense is virtually non-existent.

The mainstream military forces find themself torn between gaining for the fruits of the information revolution when applied to the traditional concepts of military roles and missions and finding themself riding the back of a tiger that might threaten to overturn those traditional concepts and replace them with a new kind of war and warrior. The balancing act is how to embrace the information technologies without being institutionally undone by them. Whether the choice is real or not may be less pertinent than the fact that there are factions within the military forces that are willing to make the choice seem real to those in and out of uniform who must decide how the military should be organised and funded. That such opposing views might surface within the military and be broadcast is certainly not without precedent, but the information revolution has just as certainly made the debate more visible and widely spread. So, one important fallout of the information revolution is the looming prospect of information warfare—warfare waged with information as a primary weapon or target. Although information warfare as a component of war is not new, the possibility that it might become the dominant dimension in future war is new. That possibility looms now because of the growing dependence on information infrastructures for the most modern means of warfare and for the economic functioning of a modern society and state. Even those in the military forces who believe information warfare is the wave of the future find themselves pulled between complementary interests and concerns:

i) The interests are the potential military advantages of exploiting information as a weapon against the entire range of enemy targets—from the minds of the enemy's leadership to the performance of their weapons.

ii) The concerns are the potential vulnerabilities of the sophisticated civil and military infrastructures—communications, commercial, logistical, and command—to hostile actions using information as a weapon.

The idea of information warfare will take a longer time to mature than its most ardent proponents expect and, in the near term, will probably deliver less than it promises. But there is also something unique about the information revolution compared to the previous technological revolutions in the twenteinth century, with differences that could break the observable patterns of the past. Unlike the prior technical revolutions in this century, the information revolution is dramatically altering the power relationships between the state and society, not just in America or even the developed world, but throughout the globe. And it is from the state that the military draws its mandate. While the revolution wrought by the internal combustion engine gave Americans wheels and wings, the relative power of the state to the individual only increased as society looked to the state for the needed roads and airways. Nuclear power and space were, for the most part, state-managed monopolies that did not involve relinquishment of state power to individuals.

But the information revolution has unleashed forces—both political and economic—that have significantly eroded the relative power of the state with respect to individuals and all sorts of new non-state actors. Sovereign powers that states took for granted even two decades ago—such as control over their borders, markets, currency, information, and population movements—have been significantly weakened. This is not to say that the state is about to disappear—only that the powers of individuals relative to states, because of their access to information, are presently in ascendancy.

The most powerful engine of change in the relative decline of states and the rise of non-state actors is the computer and telecommunications revolution, whose deep political and social consequences have been almost completely ignored. Widely accessible and affordable technology has broken governments' monopoly on the collection and management of large amounts of information and deprived governments of the deference they enjoyed because of it.

Even the ability of the state to wield military power with the freedom that its elites might prefer has been greatly circumscribed by the information revolution—a fact the military forces has come to appreciate throughout the last half of the twenteinth century when it talks about (a) "the CNN effect", through which military operations are increasingly exposed to news-media examination, (b) the political imperative to hold casualties to a minimum to retain public support, and (c) planning in the face of political constraints on the use of force. These were not significant considerations in the first half of the 20th century, before the information revolution.

Much of the current focus of the military forces on information warfare—offensive or defensive—is on applying the burgeoning information technologies as new tools for what it sees as its traditional mission of fighting and winning the wars. The military mission is still fighting and winning the wars, but those wars will now be fought with some new tools and in new ways. Information warfare is one of those new ways, and the information technologies will provide many of the new tools. The problem with that formulation is that the information technologies are driving much more fundamental changes elsewhere—transforming societies and their institutions, creating new and destroying old enterprises.

The military forces may assume that their enterprises remains unchanged, despite the ravaging effects of the information revolution on the powers of the nation-state and the transformation of entire societies, economies, and enterprises everywhere. If so, the principal effect of the information technologies on the military forces will be limited to their application in the existing enterprise. However, the effects of applying the information technologies as new tools in old enterprises has almost everywhere proved disappointing—in business, governance, and education-because the dramatic changes wrought by the information technologies are to be found elsewhere in the societal changes that are producing new values, expectations, aspirations, and enterprises. When businesses automated their old accounting or inventory processes, they found themselves disappointed with the cost savings. Computers introduced into the classroom have had little visible or measurable effect on the traditional enterprise of education. Managers everywhere see the movement of greater amounts of information through computer networks but only modest improvements in productivity.

By applying the information technologies to its old enterprises—whether that be digitising the battlefield or preparing to engage in interstate information warfare—the military forces could be diverted from the more important and difficult task of anticipating and reshaping itself to undertake new and different enterprises. The challenge for the military forces is to anticipate what those new enterprises may be before it is confronted with the tasking.

DIGITISED BATTLEFIELDS

Digitising the battlefield may make soldiers more effective or efficient on battlefields as they were understood in the twentieth century, but it may add less than expected to the tasks that lie ahead for the American military in the twenty-first century. The ability to wage interstate information warfare—offensive or defensive—may or may not be salient to the new world that is now emerging for the military forces.

Offensive information warfare as it is currently conceived may be salient only if being prepared to wage interstate warfare remains the principal enterprise for the military forces in the twenty-first century. Offensive information warfare directed against an entire society or community may be the province of the military, but that may be rarer than information attacks upon individuals or small groups where the advantage of the military over individuals is less evident. In offensive information warfare, the differences in capabilities between the military and an individual may be much less than they are in the applications of physical force.

Defensive information warfare may turn out to be the distributed burden of society every bit as much as its military—where all who use the fruits of the information revolution, civilian or military, must look after their own protection. Just as state-sponsored terrorism has brought about responses with military strikes, so too state-sponsored information attacks might bring about responses in the form of physical force. Where information attacks come from individuals or non-state actors, it is not at all clear that the military forces would be involved unless its own infrastructures were the target.

To anticipate what the future enterprise of the military forces may be in the early twenty-first century, it may be helpful to look at its past enterprises during the twentieth century. This century has seen the military forces preoccupied with at least six different enterprises at different times, sometimes reverting to an earlier enterprise. At any given time, several of these six enterprises were usually detectable, but only one at a time, dominated the American military as its primary purposeful activity. The six enterprises are as follows:

i) Providing constabulary capabilities.
ii) Mounting an expeditionary force.
iii) Keeping the military arts and sciences alive.
iv) Providing a deterrent.
v) Providing a forward defence.
vi) Providing a global presence.

These six enterprises constitute the past, but they do not exhaust the possibilities for the future. At least two other purposeful enterprises have lurked during the twentieth century:

i) Defending the homeland.

ii) Maintaining a mobilisation base.

As the twentieth century closes, it is clear that the enterprise of the military forces is being prepared to mount an expeditionary force.

The enterprise will change because of the information revolution's transformation of societies and economies and, hence, the nature of conflict—the subsidence of nation-state warfare with regular forces and the rise of non-state and intrastate conflicts brought about by the globalisation of information and commerce. If so, the enterprise might shift toward providing constabulary capabilities for a more disorderly world or, alternatively, toward defending the homeland from terrorists, criminals, and rogues. Another possibility, raised by those looking to a revolution in military affairs instigated in large part by the information revolution, is a return to circumstances similar to the interlude between the two world wars, "largely peaceful decades but also periods of change and debate in military technology and strategy."

IW STRATEGIES

Dealing with information-warfare threats requires a different approach, one that merges the external and internal threats. Table 1 summarises the main strategy to be used against each adversary; it should be emphasised, however, that these strategies supplement each other in all cases and need to be used in combination. In any serious defence strategy to deal with the information-warfare threat, local and national protection must be emphasised first.

Developing a comprehensive prevention strategy requires facing up to some serious legal, strategic, organisational, and policy challenges. Eliminating vulnerability is always preferable to managing threats. However, protection alone is unlikely to be sufficient. Therefore, it must be accompanied with plans to prevent and deter attacks. Prevention should be emphasised as the primary strategy for the middle-level threats that are most imminent. For the highest end of the threat spectrum, a deterrence strategy to defend against weapons of mass disruption by a major power is likely to become essential.

Table 4.1
Information warfare: actors and strategies

Type of actor	*Subtype*	*Main strategies*
Individuals	Hacker "gray hats"	Protection, deterrence
	Criminal "black hats"	Protection, deterrence, prevention
Coordinated substate groups or networks	Ad hoc	Protection, deterrence, prevention
	Criminal	Prevention, deterrence, protection
	Terrorist (political)	Prevention, protection
	Terrorist (millennial)	Prevention, protection
	Insurgent	Prevention, protection
	Commercial organisations	Prevention, protection
States	Small	Prevention, deterrence
	Peer	Deterrence

The "battlespace" associated with IW has been a constantly expanding one, moving far beyond traditional military situations. In some quarters, IW has even been associated with the leveraging of information technologies to achieve greater effectiveness and efficiency. This has stretched the meaning of IW to the breaking point and has sowed more confusion than enlightenment. For this reason, this treatment of the subject uses the term "information strategies" to refer to the recognition and utilisation of information and information technologies as an instrument of national power that can be independent of, or complementary to, military presence and operations. Defending against information attacks has a number of characteristics in common with societal efforts to combat disease, drugs, and crime. Noting these similarities helps to put this problem into perspective, provides some potential useful lessons learned, and serves as a benchmark.

VULNERABILITY OF STRATEGIC INFORMATION WARFARE (SIW)

The potential impact of the information revolution on the vulnerability of key national infrastructures and other strategic assets may, over time, give rise to a wholly new kind of information-centric strategic warfare on wholly different time lines, worthy of consideration independent of other potential facets of strategic warfare.

Under normal circumstances, SIW might develop in something like the following stages:

1. *First-Generation SIW:* SIW as one of several facets or components of future strategic warfare, the latter broadly conceptualised as being carried forward through the orchestration of a number of strategic warfare instruments,
2. *Second-Generation SIW:* SIW as a freestanding, fundamentally new type of strategic warfare spawned by the information revolution, possibly being carried out in newly prominent strategic warfare arenas (e.g., economic) and on time lines (e.g., years versus days, weeks, or months) longer than those generally, or at least recently, ascribed to strategic warfare.

For established powers and emerging regional powers, first-generation SIW is the more likely form to be initially manifest.

This, however, is an arguable proposition. The United States, for example, might find itself in a situation in the near future where it chooses to exploit its current information-technology advantages and employ second-generation SIW to prevail in an international situation that otherwise would have led to troop deployments, a long campaign, and almost certain high casualties. For less-developed nations—which may not possess any other effective strategic warfare instruments—second-generation SIW may be more immediately attractive. In fact second-generation SIW use by or against lesser powers might follow close on the heels of the demonstration of first-generation SIW.

The essential infrastructures, whose incapacity or destruction would have a debilitating impact on the defence or economic security are: information and communications; physical distribution; energy; banking and finance; and vital human services. The vulnerabilities of, and threats to, the five infrastructure sectors are summarised below.

i) *Information and communications*: This sector is perhaps the most essential of all, acting as the 'nerves' and control for all other sectors. It is also one of the most vulnerable, both to physical attacks on key nodes and switches and to 'cyber' attacks through the network itself. The sheer redundancy of the interlinked networks this sector comprises may be reduced somewhat by the new competitive environment. The public telephone network is extremely complex and interrelated, governed by no single body, and evolving rapidly in time. There is, therefore, no model or simulation that accurately captures its richness; hence, it is difficult to analyse its multifarious failure modes, cascading effects, and the like. As a whole, it has proved quite resilient to periodic natural disasters, but its survivability in a coordinated, repetitive attack by a knowledgeable, determined adversary is unproven and probably unknown.

Vulnerabilities of this sector include switches susceptible to software-based disruption; a transport architecture based on synchronous optical networks, which are remotely managed through packet data network connections that are vulnerable to electronic intrusion; signalling systems based on the signalling system protocol; and control signals in an 'advanced intelligent network' design that allow changes to be made from remote locations to switch software. Some signals can increasingly be sent from private branch exchanges to control portions of the operation of the network.

The threat to these systems may arise from five categories of 'bad actors':

i) incompetents, hackers, and disgruntled employees;
ii) crooks and organised crime;
iii) political dissidents and terrorist groups;
iv) adversaries conducting foreign espionage, tactical counter-measures, and orchestrated tactical information warfare; and
v) adversaries seeking to achieve major strategic disruption.

In all sectors, the worst threat comes from the trusted insider, who already possesses physical access, knowledge of systems and procedures, and relevant passwords and system access.

ii) *Physical distribution*: This sector includes roads and highways, trucking companies, personal vehicles, railroads, airline operations, seaports and inland river terminals, oil and natural gas pipelines, and delivery services. At present, this 'system' is quite robust because of its geographic dispersion, manual procedures in place to handle problems, and multiple options that are often available for physical transportation between sites. Within the next five to 10 years, however, the picture darkens. Increased use of commercial off-the-shelf software and hardware and shared use of communication networks create additional opportunities for "trapdoors" or other implanted devices in software or hardware.

Although attacks against transportation systems account for about 20 per cent of all terrorist attacks, no tested and effective means exist that facilitates reporting and transfer of information between the government and transportation infrastructure stakeholders on threats and attacks. In addition, one can easily imagine scenarios when individual railheads, shipping points, or air traffic control centres are crucial for shipment of specific items of ammunition and material, or for units being deployed.

iii) *Energy*: Energy production and distribution systems, including electricity and oil and natural gas systems, are perhaps the second most important and ubiquitous infrastructure, along with information and telecommunications. Recent widespread multistate electric outages in the northeast and on the west coast, illustrating cascading effects during a failure, provide little comfort. Increasingly, energy industries are introducing industry-wide information systems based on open-system architectures, centralised operations, increased communications over public telecommunications networks and remote maintenance. In addition, Supervisory Control and Data Acquisition (SCADA) systems are vulnerable because of use of commercial off-the-shelf (COTS) hardware and software, connections to other company networks, and the reliance on dial-back modems that can be bypassed. As a result, significant disruption would result if an intruder were able to access a SCADA system and modify the data used for operational decisions, or modify programmes that control critical industry equipment or the data reported to control centres.

iv) *Banking and finance*: Of all the infrastructure systems, the banking and finance system is clearly the most protected and the one for which security and sustainability are extremely high priorities. Nevertheless, as with other sectors, there is danger from a subverted or disgruntled insider working for a malevolent group or nation-state. This is also possibly the place to mention a one-time threat, but one not unique to this sector: the fact that many of the complex information systems serving this sector and its affiliated organisations must be updated to handle the so-called Year 2000 (Y2K) software problem associated with the turn of the century. The problem is widespread enough that source code for these essential systems is being accessed, viewed, and manipulated by consultants, temporary employees, and other organisations, since information operations internal to banks, stock exchanges, etc., may not have sufficient resources to handle the task in addition to their normal jobs.

v) *Vital human services*: This sector includes water-supply systems, emergency services, and government services. These services are highly localised, not forming a strongly interconnected national infrastructure. Failures are therefore likely to be localised. However, because of their importance, failures can have significant psychosocial effects. Communication of vulnerabilities and threats in this sector requires cooperation among thousands of state, county, and city departments, as well as federal agencies.

POLICY DECISIONMAKING FRAMEWORKS

New strategy and policy decisionmaking frameworks are born in the crucible of necessity when a specific problem area appears to demand action and is of such a character that no readily applicable decisionmaking framework is available to forge an implementable action plan. In some situations, there may be an older candidate decisionmaking framework that has been tested for its applicability to the needs of the subject problem area and found wanting. Those who favour formulating the subject area as a rapidly evolving old problem area verses a new problem area may in fact have championed use of such an older framework. Failed attempts to apply an older decision-making framework may even have contributed to a delay in the more forthright expression of the need for a new framework.

An initial search for a single, temporally stable framework to serve the stated function for SIW soon led to the conclusion that the concept of a single framework at this stage of development was illusory. Rather, the correct construct for responding to a new strategic warfare component—one truly worthy of the label strategic rather than being just another "strategic warfare wannabe"—would have to be dynamic, capable of responding to ongoing changes in both the international security and information-technology environments. The correct construct would in fact have to be:

i) an evolving series of frameworks, recognising and accepting the "punctuated equilibrium" realities of convening and executing strategy and policy decisionmaking processes, and
ii) a process that recognises and supports the dynamic and highly evolutionary character of such a construct.

A clear and primary objective in this conceptualisation of the SIW decisionmaking framework problem is that the initial formulation of such a framework be one that can in fact evolve in response to changes in its environment—that it have an evolutionary potential rather than being merely a temporary expedient to get decisionmaking going but not have much utility thereafter.

The absence of a precursor framework in this issue area also means that the initial version of the framework will attract attention from stakeholders interested in the future of the information revolution and, of course, from the media. With this perspective in mind, the process of designing an associated inaugural first-generation SIW decisionmaking framework—a generic process that in fact constitutes the framework—can be divided into the following distinct steps.

i) *Key Dimensions of the SIW Environment:* Gain an understanding of the key dimensions of the future first-generation SIW 'environment' or 'battlespace', i.e., the dimensions of that environment that might in principle be shaped or influenced by effective near-term strategy and policy decisionmaking. Achieve this objective by:
   a) identifying the principal defining features of first-generation SIW within a spectrum of plausible first-generation SIW contexts, and
   b) selecting from among them the features that might be cast as key dimensions amenable to change as described above.

ii) *Key strategy and policy issues:* Identify those key strategy and policy issues and other issues, such as organisational issues, germane to the first-generation SIW problem.

iii) *Current state of first-generation SIW:* Assess the current state of first-generation SIW in terms of absolute and relative offensive and defensive SIW capabilities.

iv) *Alternative first-generation SIW 'end states':* In the light of the above-cited first-generation SIW contexts and scenarios, craft a set of alternative first-generation SIW 'end states'—expressed in terms of the above key dimensions of the first-generation SIW environment.

v) *Alternative action plans:* Array the key SIW strategy and policy issues against each of these alternative end states and conceptualise action plans for moving toward one or more of these end states.

Any such framework will need continual testing and evaluation against emerging contingencies. It should be recognised, however, that it may be hard to achieve a sustained high comfort level with respect to the viability of any framework until the related information technology and international security environments are less dynamic. It is anticipated that a second-generation SIW framework would have generic steps similar in character to those presented for first-generation SIW, but no attempt has been made to craft such a framework, not least because of the highly uncertain character of a second-generation SIW campaign.

The key dimensions of the SIW environment are obtained by identifying the defining features of the SIW environment and asking which of these can be potentially shaped or influenced in some favourable direction by well-conceived strategy and policy decisionmaking. These dimensions thus constitute the basic factors in the SIW setting that influence attainable objectives relating to SIW and the relationships between purposive action by states and changes in the shape of the SIW environment itself.

SIW presents a broad and complex spectrum of issues and challenges to existing decisionmaking processes. As a consequence, it is clear that some sequencing is appropriate in taking up these issues nationally and internationally.

A macro-assessment of the current state of first-generation SIW in terms of absolute and relative offensive and defensive SIW capabilities nations would be difficult to do even at a classified level. The current dynamic character of the information revolution and the embryonic character of SIW as a potential political-military instrument both argue for caution in making such an assessment—classified or unclassified—now and for the foreseeable future.

Offensive first-generation SIW, which by definition has the potential to hold at risk a country's central nervous system, is a much more sensitive undertaking than are "information operations" as supporting missions in conventional warfare. It is one thing to target military leadership, communications, and radar; it is quite another to target public utilities that, among other things, provide power to hospitals.

While a great deal of uncertainty surrounds the future vulnerability of information infrastructures, it can be observed that a number of trends seem to point toward an expanded dependence on inherently less-secure networking concepts. In particular, the widespread adoption of open network standards and technologies means that the industries and applications delivered via cyberspace may become more vulnerable to single-point failures. The growth of electronic commerce, the prospective expansion of electronic stored value payment systems, and plans for the delivery of critical services over the global information infrastructure all present potential targets for an SIW attack.

The defensive SIW assessment thus comes down to an assessment of information-infrastructure vulnerability, threat potential, and vulnerability consequences. These assessments also have problems. Existing information infrastructure systems are complex, dynamic, flexible, and interdependent. They are public and private, military and commercial. Some have been "hardened" by design because of the potential risk and cost of compromise. Others have evolved in a more benign environment with non-threat forcing functions. Standard risk assessment methodologies have uncertain applicability and future analysis potential because information systems are very complex and because threats can be very diabolical. Information security responsibilities are decentralised, and specific system vulnerabilities that are discovered are very sensitive and tightly held. Undiscovered risks may continue to be the greatest concern. This suggests that continuing vigilance is required so that known problems can be fixed as they are discovered. If known problems are hidden but not fixed, threats can be monitored and contingency plans can be developed, but associated risks may be impossible to measure in terms of direct loss potential.

IW DEFENCE

While eradicating information attacks, significant progress can be made in defending against all forms of information attacks, enough so that the risks can be kept at acceptable levels. Defending, as it is used here, includes preventing attacks, blunting attacks, and controlling the damage caused by attacks. The problem of IW Defence (IW-D) is similar to the problems encountered in the "wars" on disease, drugs, and crime in a number of dimensions.

i) The solution to any of these problems requires the efforts of a number of organisations, both public and private.

ii) It is unlikely, given the competition for resources, that any of these efforts will be fully funded. Therefore, we can expect that there will never be what those who have IW-D responsibilities think are a sufficient level of funding for IW-D programmes.

iii) These are not static problems. Drug cartels and criminals certainly learn from their mistakes. Even viruses "learn". Thus, defence forces will be continuously locked in a battle to keep up with attackers.

iv) Public awareness and concern will reach peaks, often accompanied by frenzied efforts to solve the problem. These relatively short periods of interest will be followed by longer periods when the urgency to solve the problem will give way to apathy. Maintaining funding and progress during these periods of waning public interest will be one of the key challenges of leadership in this area.

v) Organisations and individuals will learn to make adjustments in their behaviour to deal with IW attacks and their often unintended consequences. These adjustments will be made so that those organisations and individuals can accommodate some level of pain—a dynamic equilibrium of sorts—as the cost of doing business in the information age.

vi) Solutions will, of necessity, involve compromises. This is due to the natural tensions that exist among the various stakeholders.

The power of information was clearly demonstrated in the context of traditional conflict. Information was leveraged to significantly improve the effectiveness of all aspects of warfare from logistics to command, control, communications, and computers, intelligence, surveillance, and reconnaissance (C4ISR). Digital war, enabled by advances in technology and its widespread adoption as well as the globalisation of economics and commerce, is surely a strategy that potential adversaries are thinking about to achieve some of the objectives that have previously been sought by means of traditional warfare. It threatens the ability of a nation state's military to interpose itself between its population and "enemies of the state", thereby causing a loss of sanctuary.

Attacks of this sort, particularly when they consist of more than an isolated incident, create a perception of vulnerability, loss of control, and loss of confidence in the ability of the state to provide protection. Thus, the impact can far exceed the actual damage that has occurred. This non-linear relationship between actual damage and societal damage makes the problem of digital war a particularly challenging one because it creates a mismatch between rational defence responses and their effectiveness.

Responding to these attacks with traditional military forces may be politically unacceptable or in fact, may be ineffectual. Currently there is no consensus, even among those in the defence establishment who think about these issues, regarding how to deal with such an attack. Given the potential effectiveness of digital war, particularly as an instrument of power for niche competitors and non-state actors, we need, as a society, to take this information age form of war very seriously.

As far as security considerations are concerned, five points need to be made.

i) This issue is not whether or not an attack could totally destroy or disrupt a particular system or type of service, but whether or not there could be sufficient damage to trigger the perception of a failure and result in panic behaviour that could in turn create a significant national problem.

ii) The redundancies in the systems are only partial and unplanned. Hence, they are neither complete nor reliable.

iii) The legacy systems, many having been designed and built with little or no attention to security, are difficult to protect and secure.

iv) As the need for interconnectivity and interoperability increases, more and more systems are being lashed together with "work-arounds". These patches, in many cases, compromise security.

v) The lack of security that these systems provide is dampening the demand for services that could make operations more effective and efficient in many areas.

In IW-D, working to formulate the problem accomplishes three things:

i) It provides a useful framework for discussion.

ii) It serves to keep the focus on those specific areas that are either unknown or in dispute.

iii) It serves as a benchmark for measuring progress.

The states of nature correspond to the nature of the threat that will be faced *vis-a-vis* the vulnerabilities of our information infrastructure while our options correspond to the strategies we adopt and the actions we take to defend ourselves. The objective being sought corresponds to a level of infrastructure performance, its definition and measure being a major challenge in and of itself. A good place to start is to try to develop an understanding of the nature of the threat, or more accurately the spectrum of relevant threats. This involves the identification of potential threats and the estimation of their likelihoods. Normally one would construct a set of states of nature that are mutually exclusive and collectively exhaustive so that a probability density function could be used.

The threat we face is multidimensional, somewhat messy and, with respect to the consequences of information attacks, can behave in a chaotic manner. The dynamic and interactive nature of the threat makes defending against attacks all the more challenging. Attackers and defenders are locked in an ongoing battle of wits and resources. Unfortunately, the attackers possess some inherent advantages. For example, the attacker can pick the time, place, medium, and method of the attack. The technology edge also goes to the attacker, for it is very difficult to develop perfect defences at an affordable cost. Therefore, there will always be "holes". Which ones will be exploited are unknown until attacks occur, thus the offence usually is one step ahead of the defence.

Collection and analysis of information about attacks is vital to maintaining parity with attackers. The problem of how best to defend against a variety of potential digital information attacks is exacerbated by the following three characteristics of the problem: our inability to develop a simple relationship between a type of attack or threat and an organisation, the essentially non-linear relationship between outcome and value, and the fact that key variables are not within our control.

The problem of IW-D resists decomposition along organisational lines. This is because there is a weak mapping between threat and organisation from two perspectives. First, the organisational target of the attack is weakly related to the threat topology, that is, an attack on a given organisation may result in a set of consequences that span the threat spectrum. Second, there is no clean mapping between organisational responsibility and the threat topology. It is always easier to solve problems with well-behaved or predictable objective functions or measures of value. The IW-D problem has situations where the relationship between events and variables behave in a chaotic manner. This introduces a large dose of uncertainty into the equation. If these first two characteristics of the IW-D problem did not present significant challenges in and of themselves, we are also faced with the fact that some of the key variables that have an influence on outcomes and the values of these outcomes are only partially controllable.

For anyone who thrives on challenges, defending against information warfare is a great line of work. There are five key challenges we face.

The first challenge involves the development of a better understanding of the nature and characteristics of the threat among society and its institutions. Success requires that everyone be on board. Therefore, it is important that we continue to work to increase awareness of this problem and to develop a better understanding of both the nature of the threat and our vulnerabilities.

The second challenge is to develop a strategy for deterring digital information attacks. The first line of defence is deterrence. Not enough effort is being devoted to developing and gaming possible strategies.

The third and fourth challenges involve developing means of providing warning for attacks and ways of successfully defending against attacks that do occur. Improving our ability to see an attack coming, or providing indications and warning (I&W) of attacks in a timely fashion, is perhaps the most single difficult challenge we face. Developing an IW capability involves not only the traditional strategic and tactical warning capabilities, but also the ability to know that an attack has begun and to ascertain the likely scope of such an attack.

The fifth challenge is to develop appropriate and effective responses to such attacks. Responses to attacks include identification, interdiction, apprehension, and punishment.

IW differs from atomic warfare in a number of significant ways, and therefore lessons learned from our experience in developing a workable strategy for deterrence may not apply directly to the problem of deterrence of IW attacks, but certainly may provide a starting point or checklist for consideration. Some of the compelling issues related to the development of a deterrent to IW attacks include various means of raising the attack threshold, using offensive IW, dealing with non-state actors, taking pre-emptive actions, and developing potential forms of punishing attackers. While raising the defensive threshold, thereby making attacks more difficult and costly as well as limiting the damage they can do, is widely recognised as an important component of any deterrence strategy, an issue that needs to be addressed relates to the "height" of the threshold. Another critical issue is whether or not having and indicating a willingness to employ a potent offensive IW capability would be an effective deterrent, and if so, in which particular set of circumstances.

In order to achieve the requisite level of defences, we need to:

i) revise our approach to system design and acquisition,

ii) understand the dimensions of defence, and

iii) support the development of critical enabling technologies.

The current trend in designing systems is to provide vastly increased access to increasing amounts of information at all levels of an organisation and to provide for more external connectivity. Driven by the reduced lifecycle of information technology and shrinking budgets, we are becoming more and more reliant on commercial-off-the-shelf (COTS) equipment and software. These trends make it more and more difficult to ensure the integrity of information or recognise when it has been compromised.

In evaluating system designs and in setting standards for systems to meet, we need to augment the current set of measures of merit (MOMs) for information. In addition to attributes such as timeliness and accuracy, we also need to focus on authenticity, integrity, and availability. Connectivity is important to achieving the levels of functionality desired, but increased emphasis on secure interoperability is needed to achieve IW-D objectives. Fixing and patching systems and installing new releases offer many opportunities to bypass or disable system defences. Operations and Maintenance (O&M) activities also provide opportunities to prevent intrusions and strengthen system defences. System operators and software maintenance engineers are often the least experienced and lowest paid in their professions.

Many of the defensive capabilities we currently have are not adequate for certain known levels or types of attacks, not to mention technically feasible but undocumented attacks. The cornerstone of the efforts to combat IW will be the efforts of all organisations to protect their own systems and information. Some organisations have been worrying about this for a long time and have developed and implemented plans to keep on top of this increasingly serious set of threats.

A few organisations may find that IW-D adds a mission or increases the importance of an existing mission. New relationships with external organisations may be required, or perhaps existing relationships may need to be modified. Thus, a review of these relationships is in order. Perhaps the organisation has a Chief Information Officer (CIO) and it would be appropriate for the CIO to take on this responsibility. Perhaps the responsibility for IW-D is spread out among several individuals. Not all information or all systems should be considered equal with respect to the protection they merit. It is important, given resource constraints, to identify which information and systems are critical and which are not critical.

REFERENCES

Ashman, Bruce W., "Defensive Information Warfare in Today's Joint Operations: What's the Real Threat?", *Strategy Research Project*, Carlisle Barracks: US Army War College, 7 April 1997.

Buchan, G. C., *One-and-a-Half Cheers for the Revolution in Military Affairs*, Santa Monica, Calif, 1997.

Cook, Wyatt C., "Information Warfare: A New Dimension in the Application of Air and Space Power", *Selected Essays- Air War College Class of 1994,* Maxwell AFB, AL: June 1994.

Cooper, Pat, "Information Warfare Sparks Security Affairs Revolution", *Defense News* 10, pp.1, 66, 12-18 June 1995.

Dearth, Douglas H., "Information War: Rethinking the Application of Power in the 21st Century", *Military Intelligence* 23, pp.11-16, January-March 1997.

Department of Defense. *Information Warfare*, DOD Directive TS3600.1. Washington DC: 21 December 1992.

Department of the Navy, *Policy Planning and Guidance for Naval Information Warfare/Command and Control Warfare.*, Washington DC: 16 Feb. 1995.

Department of the Air Force, *Cornerstones of Information Warfare,* Washington, D.C.: Department of the Air Force, 1995.

Hopper, William Frank., *Command and Control Countermeasures Doctrine in the Naval Environment,* Monterey, CA: Naval post-graduate School, June 1983.

Hutcherson, Norman B., *Command and Control Warfare,* Maxwell AFB, Alabama: Air University Press, 1994.

Keegan, John, *The Second World War,* New York: Viking, 1989.

Mahnken, Thomas G., "War in the Information Age", *Joint Forces Quarterly*, pp. 39–43, Winter 1995–1996.

Molander, Roger C., Andrew S. Riddile, and Peter A. Wilson, *Strategic Information Warfare: A New Face of War*, Santa Monica, Calif., 1996.

Morton, Oliver, "Defence Technology: The Information Advantage", *Economist* 335, 10 June 1995.

Nichiporuk, Brian, and Carl H. Builder, *Information Technologies and the Future of Land Warfare*, Santa Monica, Calif., 1995.

Schwartau, Winn, *Information Warfare: Chaos on the Electronic Superhighway*, New York: Thunder's Mouth Press, 1994.

Sun Tzu, *The Art of War*, trans. Thomas Cleary, Boston, Mass.: Shambhala Publications, distributed by Random House, 1988.

Toffler Heidi and Alvin, *War and Anti-War: Survival at the Dawn of the Twenty-First Century*, New York: Warner Books, 1993.

Ward, Robert W., et al. "C3/Space and Electronic Warfare", *Desert Storm Reconstruction Report*, vol. VIII, Alexandria, VA: Center for Naval Analysis. June 1992.

Warden, Col. John A. *The Air Campaign: Planning For Combat*, Washington, DC: National Defense University Press, 1988.

Waller, Douglas, "Onward Cyber Soldiers", *Time,* August 21, 1995.

Williams, Robert H., "Info Warfare Attacks Score in Military's Risk Pantheon, *National Defense* 81, pp.16-17, September 1996.

Williamson, John, "Winning the Data War", *Jane's Defence Weekly* 23, pp.44-46, 20 May 1995.

5

Consequences in Society

The spread of modern information technologies has brought about considerable changes in the global environment, ranging from the speed of economic transactions, to the nature of social interactions, to the management of military operations in both peacetime and war. Governments, academic institutions, private corporations, armed forces, and individuals now share a common, global infrastructure and benefit from increased connectivity. The internet permeates and ties together infrastructures, daily operations, and security structures, in ways no other technology has before. The technology continues to change and insinuate itself into everyday life more rapidly than society's collective consciousness of it.

The effects of new information technology are all around us. Change is abundant in everything from the computers on our desks to the cell phones in our pockets. These changes offer many advantages, which leads the world in the civilian and military application of information technology. The civilian sectors all over the world already bristle with a dense information infrastructure that offers unprecedented wealth and convenience. The armed forces lead all other militaries in applying new information technologies to the problem of national defence. But technical advances are not unmixed blessings. Already, the increasing interdependence of our societal infrastructure and its concentration at unique nodes has created considerable vulnerabilities. Truck bombs against power plants, hand-held surface-to-air missiles against civil aircraft, and biological agents distributed over urban complexes are all examples of ways in which terrorists, non-national groups, small rogue states, or peer competitors can directly attack and cause significant damage.

As we wired the world and our lives, we add new vulnerabilities that will be exploited. We have no desire to stop, or even slow down, the dramatic technological improvements that the information revolution offers. None the less, as we incorporate new systems into our lives and as we become increasingly dependent upon them, we must be prepared to protect ourselves.

The new information infrastructure achieves its economic and social potential through its interconnections. These interconnections may ultimately create a single system, wiring together the entire national information infrastructure. Everyone and everything might be wired to everything else. Despite its enormous advantages, the prospect of a single system has brought to the fore the inherent defensive advantages of isolation. The previous isolation of systems meant that it was difficult to attack them remotely and that it was even more difficult to disrupt them all at the same time.

Interconnections create vulnerabilities because they create the potential for attacks, launched from afar, to threaten the economy, society, and security. Using information tools, adversaries can threaten to disrupt economic well-being by attacking key infrastructures or military operations and power projection at multiple levels. However, increased reliance on cyberspace is unlikely to make war bloodless. Disrupting the information systems can create physical damage indirectly. But attacks against our information systems need not be used alone; they can be even more effective and damaging if used in combination with some physical attacks, whether by conventional forces and/or with weapons of mass destruction.

Individual hackers or terrorists, substate actors such as criminal gangs, insurgent groups, or transitional political organisations, rogue states, and peer competitors can use these techniques in the hope of advancing their various aims. The persistence and perhaps increase in vulnerability to disruption is likely to require us to rethink our current definition of security—defences against threats mounted from abroad. Dealing with information attacks can result in some merger of the internal and external threats. This in turn will raise many fundamental organisational and legal issues.

There is likely to be increased tension between concerns about privacy and civil rights and concerns about national and personal security. It may also create new missions for the armed forces. The military already has the task of protecting its own information systems. There are a variety of ways for hostile forces to attack to information systems and new methods for such attacks are being developed. Techniques for information attack includes physical destruction, electromagnetic pulse, corruption of insiders and computer intrusion attacks.

CYBER THREATS

Well-documented incidence of cyber crime—ranging from identity theft to fraud to economic espionage to cyber extortion—have become alarmingly frequent. Establishing the source, nature, and severity of cyber threats in the dawn of their real potential is a complex undertaking. Understanding the distinctions between attacks and motives, and improving the ability to provide fast and accurate assessments of the nature of both the attacks and their perpetrators, are a core part of the problem at hand.

Extremely sophisticated information warfare (IW) tools have become freely available over the internet. Now even novice hackers can easily find system vulnerabilities that it once took years of experience and sophisticated training to detect. While counter-measures to these tools do exist, they require great expertise and awareness to implement. Indeed, machines with inadequately trained system administrators often exhibit security holes that have been widely known for years.

Given the increased reliance on computer networks in recent years, this disparity between the ease of attacks and the difficulty and delay in adopting counter-measures has led to a dramatic increase in computer crime in recent years. The global context in which these vulnerabilities reside is very complex. In contrast with the bipolar situation of the Cold War, now there are many different possible enemies in the form of individual terrorists, various coordinated subnational groups or networks, small states, and potential peer competitors.

There are the individuals who break into computer systems. These fall into two types. There are those who break in for pure pleasure, for the challenge. Although illegal, this so-called "gray hat" hacking is quite different from that carried out by "black hats," who threaten to damage for purposes of blackmail or theft of funds or information. Gray hats are criminals, but they are more akin to vandals than to thieves. Both gray and black hats can be trusted insiders who gain access through privileged information. Even though these gray and black hats are motivated by very different incentives, they share an important characteristic: They generally do not have ideological motives and have little interest in upsetting national security. However, such attackers can directly affect a nation's security if they target the security agencies or critical infrastructure.

An individual can create a "virtual mass" with widely distributed, diversely targeted and synchronised attacks. Individual attackers can indirectly threaten a nation's security if they act as "inventors" or pathfinders of disruptive measures. When led by a cause to join together for some purpose, organised gray hats may also be able to cause damage that could have more serious military consequences. Coordinated groups, therefore, present an altogether different type of threat.

The threat picture becomes more complex when one includes not only small, ad hoc groups but also dedicated organisations that gain IW expertise to attain specific goals. The

Dutch hackers who volunteered to help Saddam Hussein during the Gulf War by mounting IW attacks on the US military would certainly have been engaged in a military action on behalf of a nation-state. Such groups could also be developed or employed by terrorist groups, transnational criminal organisations, or insurgent groups. These groups or other hostile actors might hire cyber mercenaries.

Traditional states could develop and use IW techniques. It is not hard to envision, for example, that a country's secret service would have a group of intelligence officers whose goal was to employ IW techniques to gather intelligence on potential opponents, for commercial, political and military purposes. An adversary could use the approach in preparation for a possible attack using either physical or IW means.

Coordinated groups and states will likely not use solitary hackers. Rather, they will rely on coordinated and repeated attacks of deferent agents or massed attacks. They may also demonstrate the capacity to attack several sites simultaneously, denying the defender the ability to concentrate defensive resources. It is important to recognise that the coordination can be done sometime in advance and then carried out by autonomously operating attack cells. Decapitating such an organisation will therefore not eliminate its capacity to do damage. The possibility of damage from multiple, coordinated attacks exceeds the potential damage from individual attackers focused on single targets. Multiple and coordinated IW attacks would have a greater chance of overwhelming local security measures than lone individuals, unless, perhaps, an insider is involved.

The "weapons" and tools used could be very diverse and include viruses and logic bombs. Many of the tools required for information attacks are within the means of groups and even smaller developing countries.

Major regional powers or a putative peer competitor, that is, powers with a substantial information technology expertise, could eventually develop the capacity to attack a large part of, if not the entire, military and civilian national information infrastructures simultaneously. Some might emphasise military targets or civilian targets or both.

Types of Attacks

Conceptually, every information system consists of four types of components: physical systems, transmission systems, software, and data. Each component is critical to the functioning of the information system and is potentially vulnerable to either corruption or disruption. Table 5.1 lists a few types of attacks on each component, although it does not pretend to exhaust the possibilities.

Table 5.1

Information warfare attacks

Information-system component	*Purpose of attack*	*Types of attacks*
Physical component	Disable or corrupt computer hardware	Prepositioned hardware logic bombs, disruption of power supply
Transmission system	Intercept or disrupt communications	Tapping, spoofing, overloading or jamming, computer intrusion
Software	Disable, corrupt, or establish control of software functions	Prepositioned software logic bombs, exploitation of bugs, viruses, computer intrusion
Data	Destroy, steal, or corrupt computer data	Viruses, computer intrusion

Computer intrusion can be used to attack the data, software, and even transmission components of an information system.

Only the physical components are generally invulnerable to such attacks, and there are exceptions to this rule. Computer intrusions have gained prominence in recent years because the connection of so many systems to public networks, particularly the internet, has greatly expanded the available targets and the importance of the data and control functions these systems contain. Such attacks are novel because they can be perpetrated remotely and often covertly. Attackers can use a variety of means to intrude into networked computers. A few common examples from the internet world follow, but this list is far from exhaustive:

i) *Password attacks*: This is the simple expedient of guessing, or cracking through brute-force techniques, the passwords needed for entry into a computer system. Public-domain programmes exist that automatically try all possible combinations or quickly test for words using the entire dictionary. This type of attack is relatively simple to defeat, mostly by ensuring that users choose their passwords carefully. None the less, this is probably still the most common type of attack and is quite often successful in achieving entry into even sensitive computers.
ii) *Packet sniffing*: internet transmissions travel in small data packets through several intermediate hosts before arriving at their ultimate destinations. Each data packet contains the address of the sender and recipient, as well as the data being sent, which might include credit card information, personal data, or even passwords. Packet sniffers are programmes placed on intermediate hosts that intercept and examine passing data packets for interesting bits of information. Packet data can be protected by encryption. However, the hacker can still use the address of the sender and recipient as a precursor to internet Protocol (IP) spoofing. Packet sniffing is technically difficult to accomplish but is also quite difficult to protect against entirely.

iii) *IP spoofing*: Each computer on the internet is identified by an IP address. IP spoofing essentially means fooling another computer about your computer's identity by sending a fake IP address. False identification may allow the hacker to gain privileged access because the server will falsely believe the hacker to be coming from within the internal network or from another trusted network. False identification may also allow a hacker to hijack a user's communication with the server, intercepting outgoing messages and substituting his own responses. Well-con-figured systems can guard against most types of IP spoofing, but many fail even to try. Some types of IP spoofing, particularly session hijacking from within trusted networks, are extremely difficult to protect against.

iv) *Confidence games*: Hackers often exploit user naivete to gain system access. Such confidence games usually involve getting users to reveal their passwords or other personal data by claiming to be the system administrator or by providing a false log-in prompt or false website. Strict operating procedures and user education will protect against many such con games, but humans, being fallible, will always remain vulnerable to such deceptions.

v) *Exploiting software bugs*: When two computers communicate for any purpose (to exchange e-mail, to allow web-browsing, etc.), they do so through software programmes designed to allow a limited exchange of data but, at the same time, to prevent either user from performing inappropriate operations on the others machine. However, because data interchanges and allowed operations can be quite complex, many of the software programmes controlling inter-computer communications have contained serious bugs. Hackers that discover these bugs can often use them to disrupt operations, steal data, or gain control of machines with which they are legitimately entitled to communicate. Such bugs, once discovered, can usually be easily fixed. However, the fixes are often not implemented at particular sites. Moreover, because software evolves so rapidly, new problems are always emerging. Many of the most publicised hacker attacks, including the Internet Worm of 1988, have exploited these types of bugs. Internet browsers, because of their great complexity, widespread use, and rapid development, have proved, and will no doubt continue to prove, to be a rich source of such bugs.

STRATEGIES OF DEFENCE

There are three basic strategies for defence against cyber attacks:

i) protection,
ii) deterrence, and
iii) prevention.

Protection seeks to reduce vulnerability by hardening possible targets against attack, minimising the damage that such attacks can do, and increasing the ability to recover quickly. Deterrence implies reducing the incentive of other actors to engage in cyber attacks through credible threats of retaliation. Finally, prevention means hindering the ability of enemies to acquire, deploy, or successfully use IW weapons and techniques. Protection, deterrence, and prevention are all related. For example, the kind of protection needed will depend to a degree on how well one has succeeded at prevention. Protection is the preferred strategy because, if successful, it permits the psychological and political benefit of living without vulnerability. After protection, deterrence is preferred because it does not require offensive action, except after great provocation. To hinder the acquisition of undesirable capabilities, prevention must also be considered, even though it has some offensive components. To meet all threats, a successful cyber attacks defence is likely to need to use all three strategies.

Protection

Protection measures against cyber attacks can be taken at both local and national levels.

Local protection: At the local level, protection would involve steps that each potential target, military or civilian infrastructure, must take for its own security. Protection, in this context, means local defence—that is, hardening particular nodes in the information infrastructures in an effort to reduce and perhaps even eliminate vulnerabilities.

Protection involves implementing both technical and non-technical measures. Technical measures are tools used to secure information systems, akin to a lock on a door. Such tools are numerous and varied but the most common are authentication, firewalls, encryption, audit logging, intrusion detection and monitoring, virus protection, and vulnerability assessment tools. Rapid advances are being made in all of these areas, spurred by the desire of private-sector computer users to guard against crime and protect privacy. This has had the desirable side effect of enhancing the protection of national security assets. In this way, small-scale intrusions have served to spur an immune system, like response in the infrastructure that can help protect it against larger attacks. Technical protection measures get the most attention, but they are only as good as the non-technical measures that support them.

Non-technical measures refer to standard operating procedures adopted to implement technical security measures, akin to a regulation requiring everyone to lock the door behind them when they leave. Most intrusions into computer systems are not traceable to faulty technical means but rather to faulty implementations and procedures. Well-known security holes and improper password procedures persist in many computer systems despite frequent warnings. Individual computer users bear the cost of increased security measures in terms of decreased usability. They consequently tend to resist or ignore cumbersome security procedures until they have personally suffered from lax security.

Issues of procedures, behaviour, personnel selection, and monitoring as in counter-espionage can help alleviate this problem. Procedures designed to prevent and detect suspicious activity by trusted insiders are the most critical element in any protection scheme. Good technical and non-technical local security measures are probably sufficient to defend against most potential individual attackers, especially if they are not very skilled.

In theory, perfect protection is possible. In reality, it is unlikely. Local security measures by themselves may not be sufficient against determined and skilled individual attackers, organised groups, and states. Protection may not be sufficient because so many different programmes and systems are involved in today's computer implementations that, even given exhaustive security engineering, an unforeseen interaction will eventually occur. Such interactions are, in fact, so common that they have been termed "normal accidents" in other, simpler, domains. However, these systems are likely to grow even more complex as they evolve, decreasing prospects for achieving perfect security.

Individual vulnerabilities therefore will persist even with relatively good efforts at local defence. In cyberspace, moreover, individual vulnerabilities can create systemic ones. Just one poorly guarded point of entry can threaten the entire network because, having broken into one system, the intruder can have the security credentials to enter all other similar installations.

National protection: Government around the world are concerned about national protection programme to secure the nation's critical infrastructure from cyber attacks. For example, in US, the government initiated a national protection programme to secure the nation's critical infrastructure from serious attack by 2003. The programme emphasises interagency cooperation for planning, sharing information, and coordinating a government response to infrastructure attacks. It also attempts to establish a public-private partnership to allow coordinated protection of the over 90 per cent of critical infrastructure in private hands.

Deterrence

Deterrence requires several elements that are quite difficult to achieve in a cyber attacks context. First, there must be a clear declaratory policy that specifies what punishment an aggressor can expect if he carries out a particular unacceptable behaviour or attack. Next, the deterrence system must have the ability to identify an attack and the attacker, and the ability and willingness to respond in ways that cause unacceptable damage to the attacker. Finally, deterrence requires establishing the credibility to retaliate in the eyes of the prospective adversary. Given these elements, a deterrence strategy might work.

The potential for improving the ability to trace cyber attacks exists. The situation is quite bad today and is likely to present large problems for some time to come. More importantly, deterrence depends on the attacker perceiving that he can be identified. Identifying all attacks in a timely and accurate fashion is likely to remain a major problem both for deterrence and defence. Identifying smaller attacks is likely to be particularly difficult. This problem is likely to remain similar to tracing the source of terrorist attacks. This is the one area in which the problems of applying a deterrence strategy are fairly easily managed, although there may be some difficulties here as well.

Deterrence requires a potential attacker to be convinced that, if he attacks, retaliation will follow. In response to anything but the most massive disruptive attacks, there are likely to be significant problems in conveying this belief. First, there is the credibility problem. IW-like situations occur every day. Computers mysteriously fail; air traffic control systems seize; and new viruses appear. Many of these situations result from malicious activity rather than accident, although attaining complete knowledge about which is which is essentially impossible. Thus, even if we were determined to respond to every identified attack, there would still be many cases in which we did not respond, either because we regarded the situation as an accident, were not sure whether it was an accident or an attack, or could not identify the attacker.

For deterrence to be a viable strategy, the potential attacker must have strong reason to believe that he is likely to be caught and to be punished with a devastating response. Otherwise, he may blunder into an attack that brings down a devastating retaliation on his head. For effective deterrence, we must be able to convince a potential attacker that, if he were to attack us, we would know that he did it. Improving our ability to the point of high-confidence perfection in identifying the source of attacks is critical. The technical means for tracing the source of attacks are improving. But unless it improves enough that potential attackers can be convinced that they will be identified, deterrence will be problematic.

Prevention

Prevention means hindering the ability of enemies to acquire, deploy, or successfully use IW weapons and techniques. In terms of limiting the ability to acquire IW capability, the world governments currently restricts the export of some IW-related technologies, such as cryptographic systems and software, and limits the dissemination of IW-related information. However, limiting the spread of capability will be very difficult. Computer and communication technologies have already spread throughout the world. However, another important approach can be measures to prevent or limit the deployment and use of IW tools. Preventing the deployment and use of IW weapons requires having:

i) the ability to identify potential attackers
ii) a concept of warning in the IW context to determine when an IW attack is imminent
iii) an offensive IW capability both to collect information about potential attackers and to respond in a pre-emptive manner to warnings of imminent IW attack.

Meeting these requirements will not be easy. Each requirement presents major challenges.

One possible procedure for identifying attackers is to follow their traces back through cyberspace. This process involves noticing an attacker on one's system and finding the attacker's entry point into the system. To track the attacker, the defender needs access to intermediate machines that the attacker might have used while traces of the attacker are still present. Tracing an attacker back to the initial machine requires expertise on the part of system operators, organisational capacity to respond quickly to an intrusion, and international cooperation. We could train system operators to perform this backtracking, but this would place a significant new load on them. Another limitation of relying on local system administrators to backtrack is that doing so does not provide a strategic overview of the situation. Individual system administrators will have difficulty integrating information from the various different sources that would be affected in a broadly-based cyber-attack.

A national intelligence effort can provide this coordination. However, the idea of such a national intelligence effort raises many difficult legal issues, including privacy and intelligence-oversight issues. None the less, because individual system operators cannot integrate all the different information, a set of procedures would be needed to enable various national and civilian actors to interact so that effective assessments of the breadth of an attack can be made. The President's decision to expand the FBI's National Infrastructure Protection Centre (NIPC) into an interagency focal point for gathering information and coordinating a government response is an important step in this direction. However, the private sector is not participating in the NIPC. Since the private sector owns and operates much of the critical infrastructure, a way needs to be found for it to interact with NIPC. In the end, however, even national integration of this information, while an important first step, is unlikely to be enough, because cyberspace does not recognise national boundaries. Ultimately, international cooperation akin to the measures being taken at the national level might have to be considered. One of the crucial component of a prevention strategy against cyber attacks threats is the warning against the attack. Without warning, there is no possibility of pre-emption and therefore none of prevention.

IW operations alone are not good attacking ground—but they can help make opposing forces less effective. However, once a country has taken over the territory it is seeking, it might try to rely on offensive IW to deter the victim's powerful friends from getting involved to retake the occupied territory. Non-state actors may not offer traditional warning. Since such groups are organised differently from nation-states, they have fewer resources for developing traditional military options. These groups therefore are unlikely to coordinate IW with traditional military means but could combine it with physical terrorist acts.

One warning of a conventional attack is the sudden massing of troops, or an increase in the average activity level of a country's troops. Similarly, a sudden change in the amount of network traffic from a country could indicate something is about to happen. For example, an increase in internet Control and Message Protocol packets coming from a country could indicate that the country was trying to gather data about other hosts on the internet as potential targets. On the other hand, such an increase could indicate the presence of several new hosts and routers on that country's segment of the internet. Telling the difference requires other sorts of intelligence about the country's intentions. This "other intelligence" would presumably be data on the country's goals and needs-traditional targets of human intelligence-gathering. A sudden increase in the number of viruses being spread through the internet could be another indicator of possible IW attack. An opponent could conceivably use viruses to prepare the battlefield by rendering military and key civilian systems inoperable at critical times. A sudden increase in computer intrusions may provide some warning of an attack. Before such an attack could take place, any country would have to engage in extensive "intelligence preparation of the battlefield" to determine which targets were most valuable and which were most vulnerable. This information-collection process might take place over the course of a long period, but it would undoubtedly intensify after the decision for an attack had been made. In and of themselves, none of these warnings provides sufficient information for definitive action to be taken, because any or all could be symptoms of something besides potentially hostile IW intent. They must be considered in concert by someone capable of assessing the warnings from all sources.

To gain the level of certainty necessary for pre-emption, passive warnings will need to trigger a series of more active measures to determine more precisely the likelihood and source of the attack. One such active measure could be the selective use of offensive IW. When a vague warning is received that an entity might be engaged in IW activities, targeted intelligence gathering would be required to verify the information. Some of this will need to be gathered by human intelligence, and some can be gathered by signals or other technical intelligence-gathering methods. The intelligence community will need to understand that indicators of IW activity that come from such covert channels will need to be integrated with these other warning signals, perhaps in a forum outside the intelligence community.

If intelligence can provide a reasonably accurate mapping of the location and intent of a potential attacker, he can be quite vulnerable to either offensive IW or conventional attacks to disable his systems. In IW, as in modern conventional warfare, the most difficult problem is finding and identifying the target. Like all high-tech weapons, extensive training is required to use offensive IW weapons. It matters little how advanced a weapon is if its operator is not trained to use it. Untrained or inadequately trained operators make mistakes; in wartime, this costs lives.

Prevention strategies can be useful when applied against a reasonably limited set of hostile actors. The reason for this is that prevention is too information intensive to use against the large number of individuals and small groups that could conceivably threaten computer-based information systems. To be practical, a prevention strategy needs to be focused and applied selectively.

REFERENCES

Arquilla, John, and David F. Ronfeldt, *The Advent of Netwar,* Santa Monica, Calif.: RAND, MR-789-OSD, 1996.

______________, "Cyberwar Is Coming", *Comparative Strategy*, Vol. 12, No. 2, pp. 141–165, RAND, RP-223, Summer 1993.

Bob Gelman, Stanton McCandlish, *Protecting Yourself Online: The Definitive Resource on Safety, Freedom, and Privacy in Cyberspace*, HarperCollins Publishers, Incorporated, February 1998.

Campen, Alan D., Douglas H. Dearth, and R. Thomas Goodden, (eds.), *Cyberwar: Security, Strategy, and Conflict in the Information Age*, Fairfax, Va.: AFCEA International Press, 1996.

Denning, Peter J., (ed.), *Computers under Attack: Intruders, Worms, and Viruses,* Addison Wesley Longman, Inc., January 1990.

Grimes, Roger A. A., Sue Miller (eds.), *Malicious Mobile Code: Virus Protection for Windows*, O'Reilly & Associates, Incorporated, August 2001.

Petersen, John L., *Info War: The Next Generation,* Proceedings: U.S. Naval Institute 123, pp.60-62, January 1997.

McClure, Stuart, George Kurtz, *Hacking Exposed: Network Security Secrets and Solutions*, Joel Scambray, McGraw-Hill Professional Book Group, October 2000.

Schwartau, Winn, *Cybershock: Surviving Hackers, Phreakers, Identity Thieves, Internet Terrorists, and Weapons of Mass Disruption*, Avalon, New York, April 2000.

Sterling, Bruce, *The Hacker Crackdown: Law and Disorder on the Electronic Frontier*, Bantam Books, Incorporated, October 1993.

Thomas, Tim, "The Threat of Information Operations: A Russian Perspective", in Robert Pfaltzgraff and Richard Shultz, eds., *War in the Information Age: New Challenges for U.S. Security*, London: Brassey's, 1997.

Van Creveld, Martin, *The Transformation of War*, New York: Free Press, 1991.

Weible, Jack, "Vulnerable to Attack? Subcommittees Get an Earful on Threats to Information Systems", *Air Force Times* 57, pp.28, 14 April 1997.

Whitehead, YuLin, "Information as a Weapon: Reality versus Promises", *Airpower Journal* 11, pp.40-54, 1997.

6

Cyber Security Challenges

The internet is a system of networks of unparalleled complexity that is amorphous, devoid of clear parameters, and ambiguous in ownership. The growing co-dependence of public and private organisations on common systems, networks, and commercial off-the-shelf (COTS) hardware and software is creating new and challenging vulnerabilities, both tactical and strategic. The internet, by its very nature, is an unstable, immature, and insecure technology, open to abuse and exploitation. As the systems used in both public and private organisations and in the management of infrastructures increasingly migrate to web-based protocols, the potential for disruption increases. This disruption can be low-level and inconsequential on a national security scale, for example, in the case of the defacement of a personal website or a virus that clogs up e-mail inboxes. However, the disruption can also scale up to the level of interference with military communications, significant power outages, or important economic losses due to large-scale denial-of-service (DoS) attacks. Serious disruptions already have been caused by recreational hacking, hacktivism, cracking, and the malicious unleashing of viruses and DoS attacks.

NATURE OF COMPUTER-RELATED CRIME

Computer crime can be defined as any criminal act which involves one or more computers either as the object of the crime or as accessories in its commission. Computer crime can then be subdivided into computer-related crime (CRC) and computer assisted crime (CAC). In the former, the computer or its contents is the subject of the criminal act, while in the latter, the computer is merely an accessory in the commission of a crime which could have been committed by other means.

As computer-related crimes become more prevalent, an increasing need emerges to understand how these crimes vary. An understanding of the types of computer-related crimes will assist law enforcement by providing insight for investigative strategies. There are primarily four general types of computer crimes.

i) *Computer as the target*: Crimes in which the computer is the target include such offences as theft of intellectual property, theft of marketing information, or blackmail based on information gained from computerised file. These crimes also could entail sabotage of intellectual property, marketing, pricing, or personnel data or sabotage of operating systems and programmes with the intent to impede a business or create chaos in a business' operations. Unlawful access to criminal justice and other government records is another crime that targets the computer directly. This crime covers changing a criminal history; modifying want and warrant information; creating a driver's licence, passport, or another document for identification purposes; changing tax records; or gaining access to intelligence files. Techno-vandalism occurs when unauthorised access to a computer results in damage to files or programmes, not so much for profit but for the challenge. In such cases, the damage or loss may be intentional or accidental. Another crime in this category is techno-trespass, that is, "walking" through a computer just to explore. In such cases, the intruder only looks at a file, but even this violates the owner's privacy. In all of these crimes, the offender uses the computer to obtain information or to damage operating programmes. The offender commits the crime either by "superzapping" or by becoming a "super user". Becoming a super user is relatively easy for individuals experienced in computer operations, because virtually every operating system has a trapdoor that allows individuals to enter a system and declare themselves the system's manager.

ii) *Computer as the instrumentality of the crime*: In this category, the processes of the computer, not the contents of computer files, facilitate the crime. Essentially, the criminal introduces a new code to manipulate the computer's analytical processes, thereby facilitating the crime. Another method involves converting legitimate computer processes for illegitimate purposes. Crimes in this category include fraudulent use of automated teller machine (ATM) cards and accounts; theft of money from accrual, conversion, or transfer accounts; credit card fraud; fraud from computer transactions (stock transfers, sales, or billings); and telecommunications fraud.

iii) *Computer is incidental to other crimes*: In this category of computer crime, the computer is not essential for the crime to occur, but it is related to the criminal act. This means that the crime could occur without the technology; however, computerisation helps the crime to occur faster, permits processing of greater amounts of information, and makes the crime more difficult to identify and trace. Such crimes include money laundering and unlawful banking transactions, BBSs supporting unlawful activity, organised crime records or books, and bookmaking. In one case, a suspect committed murder by changing a patient's medication information and dosage in a hospital computer. Cases involving drug raids, money laundering seizures, and other arrests also have produced computers and electronic storage media containing incriminating information. Many times, the criminals encrypt the data or design the files to erase themselves if not properly accessed. In some instances, criminals even destroy the storage media, such as disks, to eliminate evidence of their illegal activities.

iv) *Crimes associated with the prevalence of computers*: The simple presence of computers, and notably the widespread growth of microcomputers, generates new versions of fairly traditional crimes. In these cases, technological growth essentially creates new crime targets. Software piracy/counterfeiting, copyright violation of computer programmes, counterfeit equipment, blackmarket computer equipment and programmes, and theft of technological equipment fall into this category of computer crime. One offence in this category occurs with relative frequency—the violation of copyright restrictions of commercial software. Initially, this offence may not seem like a serious crime; yet, the potential loss to businesses can be quite staggering.

The 1970s and early 1980s saw a number of seminal developments in the US which laid the conceptual and practical foundations for future tools for computer crime. Around 1972, the National Security Agency (NSA) spook Dan Edwards coined the term Trojan Horse, after the Greeks' ingenious scheme to end the siege of Troy. It denotes an apparently benign macro or utility with undocumented side effects which may be security violating or palpably destructive. A trapdoor denotes a back door or security loophole left in a system which can be exploited for access purposes.

In the early 1970s, the US military was sufficiently concerned about the security of sensitive information held in computer systems to mount a number of intrusion experiments. During late 1973 and early 1974, David Stryker, John Shore and Stanley Wilson of the Naval Research Laboratory subverted the Exec VIII operating system of a Univac 1108 computer using security violating Trojan horse techniques to obtain unauthorised and surreptitious access to classified information. Meanwhile, between 1972 and 1975, in a series of experiments for the US Air Force, Steven Lipner and Roger

Schell used both trapdoors and Trojans to subvert the Multics operating system into yielding up confidential information without leaving a trace.

In 1982, John Shoch and Jon Hupp from the Rank Xerox Palo Alto Research Centre (RX-PARC) reported the first experiments with Worm programmes. The aim of their work was to 'mop up' the idle time on a network of computers with useful computations in a manner transparent to the users. The worm programme replicates itself in each node of the network and activates a portion of the desired computation if the node is quiescent; if a node becomes busy its computation is suspended and withdrawn.

The first computer virus was written as an experiment by Fred Cohen in November 1983 whilst a graduate student at the University of Southern California. As distinct from worms, viruses are parasitic replicators which must attach themselves to other machine instructions in order to be executed by the processor. The first virus infection 'in the wild', by the BRAIN virus from Pakistan, was recorded in 1986.

Basic hacking, or unauthorised access, has been practised by students, computer technophiles, commercial spies and counter-intelligence services, amongst others. Their motivations include recreation, intellectual curiosity, technical challenge, freedom of information, demonstrating security flaws, gaining commercial advantage, and national security.

Hacking may also be the logical precursor to other acts of CRC described below. Some operate solitarily, others in groups. To enter a system, either an existing trapdoor must be exploited or a valid password must be found. Passwords may be obtained remotely by 'social engineering' or locally by 'shoulder surfing'; they may be guessed or systematically cracked, or discovered using password grabber or packet sniffer programmes.

Software bombs have a similar role to destructive Trojans. Planted within some mission critical software, they consist of a trigger and a payload. If the trigger is a date and/or time it is termed a time bomb, whereas if the trigger is a logical condition it is called a logic bomb. When the host application is run the trigger condition is tested and if true then the payload is activated, often with destructive consequences. It can thus be used either for sabotage or for blackmail or extortion.

Although the identification of first software bomb is not certain, a classic example occurred in 1988 when a Texas firm called IRA suffered the deletion of some 168,000 payroll records from a database. This was shown to have been caused by a logic bomb planted by an employee named Burleson which was triggered six months after he left the firm.

Unlike logic bombs which are concealed, Trojan horses need to be explicitly run by an unwitting user in order to perpetrate their hidden side effects. They can be subdivided into those that dupe the user by offering something interesting and those that masquerade as an everyday utility. An example of the former type is the Aids Trojan which was concealed on diskettes labelled "Aids Introductory Information Diskette" offering information on the human AIDS virus. The diskettes were mailed worldwide from London in December 1989, and when installed displayed a licence agreement and printed invoices for $189 or $378. Users were instructed to send the money to a fictitious PC Cyborg Corporation at an actual PO Box number in Panama, otherwise their PC would cease to function. This was no empty threat; after a variable number of power-ups since its installation the Trojan rendered the PC inoperable. At the end of January 1990, Joseph Popp was arrested by the FBI in Ohio, extradited to London and charged with 11 counts of blackmail, but was found to be mentally unfit to stand trial.

Worm programmes are replicators which do not necessarily damage information, but instead of performing useful computation as envisaged, they may simply consume system and network resources (processor cycles, memory capacity and communications bandwidth) by increasing exponentially in numbers until they render the system incapable of performing any useful work.

Being parasitic replicators, unlike worms, computer viruses must attach themselves to executable or command files, bootstrap sectors of discs, or macros within documents. Six generations of virus are now generally recognised: benign, self-encrypting, stealth, armoured, polymorphic and macro. By the end of 1996 over 8000 individual viral strains were known, but only about a dozen were 'in the wild' of which 49 per cent of infections were due to the Word Macro Concept virus first seen in 1995. As with software bombs, the trigger can be a date or a condition, and the payload can vary from the irritating to the devastating. Different infection and concealment strategies have also been recorded, including 'slow' viruses which infect only files that are being legitimately modified, 'fast' infectors which infect every file that is opened, and multipartite or 'tunnelling' viruses which exhibit a 3-stage lifecycle moving between executable file, hard disc bootstrap partition, and main memory.

INFORMATION SECURITY

As information technology has come to play an important and vital role in all sectors of society, security has become an essential component of information technology. The potential security threats and risks have to be carefully assessed in every situation and it is absolutely vital that all concerned are made aware of the threats and risks that affect them, and over which they have control.

There are three primary methods by which information systems are protected: authorisation, message filtration, and ensuring the integrity of core processes — or to put it more in terms of today's tools: good passwords, firewalls, and virus detectors.

As computers become smarter, more sophisticated, and more flexible, they will become more like us. Yet, as they become more like us, they will begin to ingest information at the semantic level from outside sources as we do, and will thus be heir to more subtle but no less problematic forms of information warfare. A large part of what makes information systems open to attack is that they contain bugs, often and pertinently referred to as undocumented features. The more experience one has with any one piece of software the more holes can be closed. Yet, even a perfect fix lasts only until the next innovation hits the system.

Some of the key factors that influence the current level of information security are: legacy systems, the threat, consciousness of the threat, operating systems, security tools, the cost of storage, the internet, and cryptographic methods.

i) *Legacy Systems*: In the old days, information systems were relatively secure by virtue of being hosted on large proprietary machines and connected to very little. What makes systems vulnerable is the shift to smaller and far more open systems coupled with the rise of networking. For many of us, small open networked systems are the here and now; for others, however, they are still in the future. Sometimes it takes a situation like the Y2K bug to remind us that while the leading edge of technology races ahead, the lagging tail may be long and thick. As people move away from closed proprietary systems, they will expose themselves to more security risk, especially in the process control sectors.

ii) *The threat*: It is extremely difficult to know what the threat to information systems actually is, and thus all the harder to know in what direction it is going. In terms of actual day-to-day threat, information warfare has remained distinctly unimpressive. Most computer crimes are internal affairs, and most external computer crimes arise, not from systematic attack, but by small groups, or, more likely, random malevolence and even curiosity run amok. Criminal enterprise tends to be responsive to opportunity with very little lag and thus a lurch upwards in the direction of computer crime seems unlikely; at worst, a gradually rising level can be expected. As for terrorism, the world's disaffected tend not to be the more computer-sophisticated and are likely to prefer violent means for the time being. Furthermore, there is a great difference between five terrorist groups taking *faux* credit for an obvious act of terror (e.g., a car bomb) and the same folks taking credit for some glitch (e.g., a telephone outage) which may equally well be an act of nature, human error, design flaw, or the result of hostile activity. The flip side of trying to gauge the changing threat is trying to gauge whether people are going to start taking computer security more seriously or not. The two are, of course, related; the greater the threat, the more likely people will take security seriousness; no threat, less response.

iii) *Operating systems*: Most of the serious weaknesses in computer systems lie with the operating system itself. In part because of its academic legacy people have been working on Unix security, in many ways, harder than they do for any other operating system. Over time, therefore, absent major changes, one might expect Unix to get more secure. Indeed, one might have imagined that Windows NT, which is based on Digital's VMS (a fairly secure system to begin with), plus another 20 years to reflect on information warfare, would be highly secure. Strangely enough, current versions are less secure than Unix and have bugs all their own. In the meantime, the web has become the focus of the computer industry's developments. In some cases, especially electronic commerce, people are paying serious attention to security. But the glitzy end of the web business — Java, ActiveX, automatic software updates, and the various plug-ins — are all carriers of great mischief from the unscrupulous.

iv) *Security tools*: Current trends in information security treat it is a problem that can be solved by adding a patch here and there. Firewalls go on the outside of one's system and are meant to filter out certain types of messages by looking at each packet and making a determination based on their ostensible purpose. Intrusion detectors look for particular activities which are characteristic of known fault patterns and then take appropriate action. Neither firewalls nor intrusion detectors are altogether reliable today, but they are getting better against a given level of threat. It is unclear whether they might go too far and make it possible for foes to instigate an anaphylactic attack, one which, using the immune system metaphor, works by overstimulating and thus setting a system's internal defensive mechanisms against itself.

v) *Cost of storage*: As the price of computer storage falls, the feasibility of archiving everything rises to the point where no one has a credible excuse for losing information. To give an example, the 17-gigabyte DVD (digital versatile disk) of the year 2000 has enough capacity to store the complete billing records of a week's worth of long-distance calls made in the United States. In sensitive environments, very fast CD-ROMs may replace writable hard disks for storing operating systems — thereby giving viruses nowhere to rest. CD-ROMs operating with zero buffer can also log everything that happens to a computer without some hacker going back and writing over the record.

vi) *The internet*: The evolution of the internet, itself, will shape the near-term information security environment. The next version of the Internet Protocol, IPv6, has provisions for many security features such as encryption, key passing, and digital signatures. Eventually IPv6 will be universal, but deployment remains slow; the greatest penetration is occurring within specific circles of universities and other leading edge sites. Several features of the internet make it particularly attractive for hackers. What should only be a near-term problem is that the Domain Naming Service, which translates names into byte-addresses is poorly protected and has little authentication capacity. Chances are the former will be fixed, and, it may also be possible to authenticate the true source of any message coming into one's system in most cases.

vi) *Cryptographic methods*: Cryptographic methods remain the most obvious tool for information security. As hardware gets faster, the processing load for encryption and authenticating messages can be expected to decline. This is obviously true if the key length stays the same, and almost as certain if measured as the time it takes to encrypt a message which takes a fixed X hours decrypt. Thus, everything else being equal, cryptographic methods will see greater use, and information security will rise. Technology remains the wild-card behind any forecasts of encryption's use. Innovations such as elliptical methods or cryptographic analysis will affect the time required to generate or break codes. Yet, very little in the last 15 years has broken the fundamental fact that increases in key length have a modest affect on the cost of making codes and a major affect on the cost of breaking them. The one joker in the deck is the prospect of quantum computing which can break the back of the prime factoring problem thereby rendering both public key encryption and digital signatures obsolete. But no one knows whether quantum computers will work.

The increasing power of hardware and the growing sophistication of software suggests a future in which silicon starts to act more like carbon: that is, computers take on more characteristics of humans while networks take on more characteristics of human organisations. Tomorrow's information systems are likely to make, or at least set the table for, more judgements than today's do. What is more, the feedstock for these judgements are likely to be information harvested from the world out there. Such applications are likely to appear among institutions that depend on reacting to an outside environment: e.g., politico-military intelligence, business sales and marketing, environmental control, or broad-scale social service functions such as law enforcement, traffic regulation, or public health. Institutions that do not react with the outside directly but may learn from external experience may develop some links with the outside world. Process control applications may never have these links, at least not directly. Yet, even process control applications may not be immune to influence.

Some websites are crafted so that their URL appears at the top of search lists generated by automatic tools. It would not be surprising to see the less scrupulous engage in many of the same fraudulent techniques of misrepresentation and lying that today's con artists do. Indeed, for a long time to come, computers will be easier to con than people will. Thus, a flow of false information on patient histories that reflect the efficacy of a licensed drug may subtly shift a system's recommendations to another one.

In order to protect the data held on a computer system, various steps have to be taken: individual users should only be able to read the information which is needed to do their job; they should only be able to modify information which is specifically their job to modify. Finally, some information should not be accessible at all for individual users, e.g., the various log records. In simple terms, information processing involves the following types of operation:

i) *Read/create/modify/delete information*: Information is 'read/created/modified/deleted' by a 'user'. A 'user' is a person or a process (e.g., a computer programme). Authorisation to 'read' information is a question of confidentiality while 'create/modify/delete' is primarily a question of integrity.

ii) *Transport (in one way or another) of information*: One of the simplest ways of 'transporting' information is the internal transport between the keyboard, the memory and the hard disk in a Personal Computer. Another is the external 'transport' of a diskette from one place to another. Information can also be 'transported' using a 'Local Area Network' (LAN) and/or a 'Wide Area Network' (WAN).

Insecure 'transport' affects both confidentiality and integrity.

iii) *Store information (on computer 'media' to keep it somewhere)*: Once the information has been 'stored' on some kind of media (diskettes, tapes, etc.), it may become the target of unauthorised activities which will have an effect on the confidentiality and/or integrity of the information.

The investigator needs to be familiar with a number of important IT Security functions and organisational matters if s/he is to be able to give advice on prevention methods and conduct investigations. Some important functions are: information classification documentation rules; administration and personnel; user identification and authorisation; logging back-up; firewalls; intrusion detection system (IDS); and incident handling. It is essential to classify the information according to the appropriate level of availability, e.g. 'open', 'confidential', 'secret' or 'top secret'. Only then will it be possible to apply the most effective security measures.

Success in information security work depends first and foremost on developing good basic working practices and establishing procedures to ensure that they are maintained. It is also important to create a security-conscious atmosphere and establish a disciplined approach. If confidential information is to be handled, it is essential that the people chosen for the job are absolutely reliable. They should be security screened to a level equal to the highest level of confidential information they are likely to be asked to work on. Access to information should be restricted to that which the individual 'needs to know' to do his job. Particularly sensitive material should be split into sections so that only authorised staff can handle each section; no member of staff should have access to all the information.

Security measures will only be effective if staff are properly trained. It is essential that they understand the problem. This can be achieved with in-house training. The individual users must be trained how to use the network, how to handle confidential information, making back-ups, etc. Employees can be taught what to do to counter certain threats, what they should not do, whom they can call and where they can get help. It is also very important to encourage employees to report incidents so that steps can be taken to prevent any further damage. New or temporary employees should be given introductory training, during which data security and data integrity can be explained. It might also be useful to consider including a clause on security and confidentiality obligations in employees' contracts. To achieve functional and cost-effective IT Security, a number of initial steps must be taken by the management:

i) *Risk analysis:* Threats and risks, acceptable or unacceptable, vary between different organisations. It is important to analyse the risks to make it possible for the management to form a policy with their security intentions.

ii) *Policy:* There must be an Information Security policy written and approved by management. It should include the main security targets, information classification principles, responsible persons, and principles to reach the targets.

iii) *Security plan:* A plan has to be made to define how the targets and the intentions in the policy document should be realised. A priority list must be set up because it may not be possible to realise everything in the policy at the same time. The plan is a living document and has to be scrutinised by the IT security officer.

iv) *Security architecture:* With the risk analysis, the policy and the plan as a base, security architecture must be chosen. Stet Security architecture is a high level description of technical security functions and organisational needs to fulfil the security demands.

v) *Implementation:* With the security architecture as a base, different security functions and products must be selected to implement the security architecture.

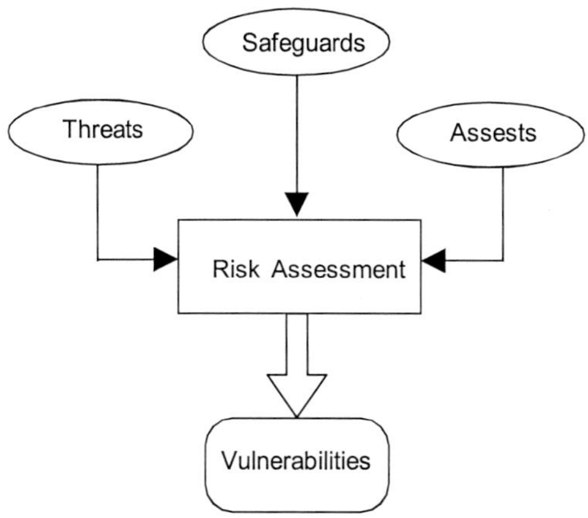

Figure 6.1: Risk assessment

Users should be given specific guidelines about what they should do and most importantly what they should not do. These guidelines should be distributed in written form, and signed for. This will counter the defence that they were unaware of the contents of the guidelines and at the same time provide the investigator with written proof. Specimen guidelines are given below. They are certainly not exhaustive and others can be added to take account of particular circumstances.

i) Do not use any computer equipment without permission.

ii) Do not try to access information unless you know you are authorised to do so.

iii) Do not alter any information on a computer system unless you know you are authorised to do so.

iv) Do not use a company or authority computer for personal matters without permission.

v) Do not leave a working computer unattended, without using security options that demand retyping a password.

vi) Make sure you know what to do in the event of a virus being discovered on the system.

vii) Use virus protection programmes.

viii) Be aware of malicious programme code, when loading files, mails etc. from the internet or other media.

ix) Keep your password and user-ID confidential.

x) Do not allow anyone else to use your password.

xi) Do not use anyone else's password.

xii) Remember that anything done on the system using your ID and password can be your responsibility.

Access to a computer can be restricted by means of controls based on various kinds of 'Identification and Authorisation' systems. Identification is a two-step function:

i) to identify the user and

ii) to authenticate the identity.

The simplest systems rely on passwords only. More sophisticated systems use cards and/or 'biometric' methods in combination with passwords.

Password systems give some measure of protection against casual browsing of information, but will rarely stop a determined criminal. A computer password acts like a key to a computer. Allowing several people to use the same password is like everyone using the same key. Passwords should be issued to an individual and kept confidential, they should not be shared with anyone.

The 'password' method is built on something you 'know' and might be misused by someone getting hold of the password. A system built on something you 'know' (password, PIN-code etc.) and something you 'have' (i.e.,, authorisation card) is a much stronger system. Even if someone gets hold of your password it is useless without the card. Today, the strongest method is something you 'know', something you 'have' and something you 'are' (biometrics). There are two main types of card:

i) *Magnetic strip card*: As its name suggests, this type of card has a magnetic strip containing some confidential information to be used together with the holder's personal code;

ii) *Chip card*: Instead of a magnetic strip, the card has a built in microchip. The simplest type contains a memory chip (e.g., telephone cards) containing some information but has no processing capability. The other, better, type is the 'active' (or 'smart') Card. It contains a microchip with both a memory to store some information and a processor. It is often used in combination with cryptographic techniques.

Biometric systems make use of specific personal characteristics of a specific person, e.g., fingerprint, voice, keystroke characteristics or the 'pattern' of the retina. Biometric systems are still quite expensive and not very common.

After identification and authentication of the user, there must be a function and set of rules to control what object (files, devices, etc.) each user is allowed to access. This is the access control system. Most computer systems have some kind of log. Even stand-alone systems sometimes have identification and authorisation systems if different users, with different authorisation levels, use them and/or when it is desirable to prevent users from using the disk drive or changing files. In a multi-user system there are always logging functions and there is often more than one kind of log. The desired level of protection will only be achieved if the various security measures are properly followed up with a log that can be analysed as and when necessary.

Although modern computer systems are generally very reliable, breakdowns and failures do occur, and users can make mistakes that lead to the accidental destruction of information. To guard against total loss of information under these circumstances, it is necessary to set up procedures for making regular copies. The information on the computer system should be copied to some form of back-up medium. This medium can then be stored in a safe place until it is needed.

For particularly valuable information several copies should be made, and each copy stored in a different place and at least in different buildings, if not different cities. The frequency with which back-ups are taken should be based on the frequency with which the information changes, the relative value of the information, and the problems its loss would cause. Regular back-up of data and system files are an essential security measure. When combined with the logging information, they should provide a comprehensive security information package.

The following guidelines may be of assistance when making back-ups:

i) Make sure that regular back-up copies are made of both data and system files.

ii) Back-up cycles should be of sufficient length to be of some use in the future. Twenty-four hour overwrite cycles are not recommended.

iii) Take a full back-up (both system and data) out of the cycle on a regular basis and archive it offsite for an extended period.

iv) Back-up tapes/diskettes should be kept in a safe place under lock and key and away from the computer and where they are secured from fire, flood, magnetic and electric fields, etc., preferably off site.

v) Periodically test the back-up to ensure that the information can actually be restored in an emergency; do not wait for disaster to strike to find the back-up system does not work.

vi) Back-ups are another important source of information for an investigator.

In many cases, the specific threats and risks to which a particular system is exposed will depend on its architecture. However there are a number of threats which can affect all systems, irrespective of their architecture. The main types of computer architecture are indicated below.

i) *Microcomputers (stand-alone)*: These computers have no facilities for permanent external communications, apart from links to peripherals (e.g., printer, scanner, streamer, extra disk drive, etc.). Nowadays it is common to have a modem and a temporary connection to the internet. This architecture is easiest to 'protect' but it is also the architecture where the users are least aware of the possible threats and risks. If it is connected to the internet it can be vulnerable to external attacks if it is not properly configured. The user is responsible for back-ups, keeping media in a safe place, protecting data from unauthorised access, etc.

ii) *Network architectures and Mini-computers*: A mini-computer is linked to several workstations to serve a limited number of users. The workstations may consist of just a keyboard and screen, or microcomputers (so-called 'intelligent' terminals) may be used. Today, these mini-computers are often referred to as 'servers' linked to their workstations through a Local Area Network (LAN). Commonly known as client-server architecture, in many organisations the old mainframe architecture is now being replaced with a number of 'servers' each of which has a different set of functions. Connections from the LAN to Wide Area Networks (WAN) are common. The user is only responsible for backing up the files on the hard disk on his own workstation (if it has one). One or more administrators are responsible for all other back-ups, loading new programmes, etc. Management of the network is normally left to a Network Administrator.

iii) *Mainframes*: Used in big organisations to serve a great number of users and/or where considerable computing capacity is needed. A special computer-room with air-conditioning is needed, too. This is often located in a restricted area of the building and specialists are required to operate the computer. Network operators monitor the communication functions and assist users if there are communication problems. System development and programming is a task for specialised staff. The user is only responsible for backing up the files on the hard disk of his workstation (if it has a disk). Due to the very fast technical development in the field of client-server it is today not possible to clearly define the difference between mainframes and servers.

iv) *Hand-held computers*: This type of computer, like personal organisers, is completely different from the others and is discussed in section 'Technical devices and communications' in the *Interpol Computer Crime Manual*. The most important prevention method is to keep the equipment in a safe place and away from unauthorised persons.

Due to exponential increases in the use of IT, there is an increased exposure to attacks on information systems, assets, and databases. However, the feared super knowledgeable computer hacker is rarely the biggest threat. Rather, the greatest dangers to computer systems and databases are "trusted" sources who often operate in the absence of even minimal attention by police and criminal justice agencies to basic IT security.

A realistic assessment of security needs and threats, followed by meaningful formulation and implementation of a security plan, can provide effective protection against the vast majority of threats, and at a reasonable cost. Many departments have made substantial financial commitments to IT. This has been accompanied by an increase in the number of reports of hacker attacks against police information systems.

The increased exposure to computer security threats is due to several causes:

i) *New business models*: The public sector is mirroring the private sector, with a delay of about five years.

ii) *Exponential growth in use of IT*: Computers and networks have insinuated themselves into almost every part of our lives.

iii) *Reduced costs*: Today's technology is inexpensive. Regardless of the metric that is used, costs for basic IT are lower than they have ever been, and the cost of new technology is decreasing faster than it did only a few years ago because of the rapid advances and increased competition.

With effective advance planning, it is possible to respond rapidly and appropriately to any attack, preventing most and minimising the impact of the rest. Overall IT planning must be done with the big picture in mind: the IT plan should flow directly from the organisation's operational plans. The plan should describe business requirements that will fulfil operational goals. Architectures should be kept simple. This provides a major security advantage.

Use of Firewalls

Security features are available in almost every commercial off-the-shelf application. Firewalls are more powerful and adaptable than ever and are very reasonably priced. Encryption programmes are becoming more powerful and easier to implement and maintain. The ability to manage and monitor distributed systems from a single point in the network is improving steadily. Automated monitoring and audit programmes to control system use and alert security administrators to attempted abuses are maturing rapidly. One of the areas of technical advance that is most promising is biometrics — the ability to identify someone based on a unique physical characteristic. Biometric devices make it possible to authenticate users more effectively than ever and will prevent unauthorised persons from accessing a system even if they possess a password.

A firewall system can enforces an access control policy between two networks. Some firewalls place a greater emphasis on blocking traffic, while others emphasise permitting traffic.

Probably the most important thing to recognise about a firewall is that it implements an access control policy. Firewall systems are typically the first line of defence between an internal network and the outside world, especially its connection to the internet. It should be configured not only to allow certain operations to occur (FTP, mail delivery, etc.), but to make it difficult or impossible for an attacker on the outside to use the firewall to penetrate the internal nets.

The main purpose with a firewall is to protect against unauthorised external attacks but it will normally leave the network unprotected from internal attacks or intrusions. The Intrusion Detection System (IDS) looks for deviations from statistical measures to detect unusual behaviour. A set of variables is defined for subject and objects such as servers, files, users and other resources, because most attacks come from inside and every company or organisation needs a well managed single point of entry as well. In addition, a firewall can keep hackers running automated intrusion programmes out of the internal network. Otherwise those programmes can detect and exploit holes in your security architecture.

Even if you have installed a firewall and an IDS someone has to take care of an incident when it occurs. Incident Handling System (IHS) is the best way to handle an incident. It is very important to stay calm and not panic when an incident occurs. It is very valuable to have a special form to register incidents. Their method has six stages: preparation detection containment eradication recovery follow-up:

i) *Preparation*: This stage covers things like policy, management supports, training and interfaces to law enforcement.

ii) *Identification*: How to identify an incident, responsible staff, co-ordination with network suppliers' etc.

iii) *Containment*: Create the on-site team to survey the situation.

iv) *Eradication*: Perform vulnerability analysis. Remove the cause of the incident, etc.

v) *Recovery:* Restore the system. Validate the system, etc.

vi) *Follow-up*: Develop a follow-up report.

Combating Computer Viruses

Viruses have become the subject of widespread urban legends and hoaxes, popular television shows and movies. Much of their popular presence is attributable to an obvious but deep biological analogy: computer viruses replicate by attaching themselves to a host (a programme or computer instead of a biological cell) and co-opting the host's resources to make copies of themselves. Symptoms can range from unpleasant to fatal. Computer viruses spread from programme to programme and computer to computer, much as biological viruses spread within individuals and among individual members of a society. There are other computer pathogens, such as the "worms" that occasionally afflict networks and the "Trojan horses" that put a deceptively friendly face on malicious programmes, but viruses are the most common computer ill by far.

Computer viruses can trace their pedigree to John von Neumann's studies of self-replicating mathematical automata in the 1940s. Although the idea of programmes that could infect computers dates to the 1970s, the first well-documented case of a computer virus spreading "in the wild" occurred in October 1987, when a code snippet known as the "Brain" virus appeared on several dozen diskettes at the University of Delaware. Today, viruses afflict at least a million computers every year. Users spend several hundred million dollars annually on antivirus products and services, and this figure is growing rapidly. Most viruses attack personal computers (PCs). More than 10,000 viruses have appeared so far, and unscrupulous programmers generate roughly another six every day. Fortunately, only a handful have been detected far afield.

There are three main classes of PC viruses (and the categories for other systems are analogous): file infectors, boot-sector viruses and macro viruses.

Roughly 85 per cent of all known viruses infect files containing applications such as spreadsheet programmes or games. When a user runs an infected application, the virus code executes first and installs itself independently in the computer's memory so that it can copy itself into subsequent applications that the user runs. Once in place, the virus returns control to the infected application; the user remains unaware of its existence. Eventually a tainted programme will make its way to another computer via a shared diskette or network, and the infection cycle will begin anew.

Boot-sector viruses, which account for about 5 per cent of known PC virus strains, reside in a special part of a diskette or hard disk that is read into memory and executed when a computer first starts. The boot sector normally contains the programme code for loading the rest of a computer's operating system (hence the name, a reference to lifting oneself up by one's own bootstraps). Once loaded, a boot-sector virus can infect any diskette that is placed in the drive. It also infects the hard disk, so that the virus will be loaded into memory whenever the system is restarted. Boot viruses are highly effective: even though there are fewer strains, they were for a time much more prevalent than file infectors were.

Macro viruses, are independent of operating systems and infect files that are usually regarded as data rather than as programmes. Many spreadsheet, database and word-processing programmes can execute scripts—prescribed sequences of actions—embedded in a document. Such scripts, or macros, are used to automate actions ranging from typing long words to carrying out complicated sequences of calculations. And virus writers have created scripts that insert copies of themselves in other documents. Macro viruses can spread much more rapidly than other kinds of viruses because many people share "data" files freely—consider several workers swapping drafts of a jointly written report. 'Concept', the first macro virus observed in the wild, infected its first Microsoft Word document late in 1995 and is now the most prevalent virus in the world.

Today more than 1,000 macro viruses are known. As well as basic replication code, viruses can contain whatever other code the author chooses. Some virus payloads may simply print a message or display an image, but others will damage programmes and data. Even those without malicious payloads can cause damage to systems whose configuration differs from what the virus designer expected.

Antivirus software has existed since shortly after computer viruses first appeared. Generic virus-detection programmes can monitor a computer system for virus-like behaviour (such as modification of certain crucial files or parts of main memory), and they can periodically check programmes for suspicious modifications. Such software can even detect hitherto unknown viruses, but it can also be prone to false alarms because some legitimate activities resemble viruses at work. Scanning programmes, in contrast, can search files, boot records and memory for specific patterns of bytes indicative of known viruses. To stay current, they must be updated when new viral strains arise, but they only rarely raise false alarms. The viral signatures these programmes recognise are quite short: typically 16 to 30 bytes out of the several thousand that make up a complete virus. It is more efficient to recognise a small fragment than to verify the presence of an entire virus, and a single signature may be common to many different viruses. Most computer-virus scanners use pattern-matching algorithms that can scan for many different signatures at the same time: the best can check for 10,000 signatures in 10,000 programmes in under 10 minutes.

Once a virus has been detected, it must be removed. One brutal but effective technique is simply to erase the infected programme, much as certain types of immune cells destroy an infected cell. Body cells are generally easy to replace, but computer programmes and documents are not so expendable. As a result, antivirus programmes do their best to repair infected files rather than destroy them. If a virus-specific scanning programme detects an infected file, it can usually follow a detailed prescription, supplied by its programmers, for deleting viral code and reassembling a working copy of the original.

Experts must identify unusual sequences of instructions that appear in the viral code but not in conventional programmes—a process that relies on carefully developed knowledge and intuition. They also must develop a prescription for verifying and removing the virus from any infected host. To keep up with the influx of half a dozen new viruses a day, antivirus technologists have developed automated tools and procedures to assist human virus experts or even replace them.

Virus hunters have learned to exploit the fact that programmers often make new computer viruses from key parts of existing ones. These viral "genes" enable us to trace the evolutionary history of computer viruses, in the same way that biologists determine the family trees of related species. By processing large collections of viral code, we can automatically derive a set of family signatures that catches all the different members of a viral family, including previously unknown variants.

A neural-network technique is also developed to recognise viruses by scanning for several, very short patterns, each only three to five bytes long. These tiny fragments represent computer instructions that carry out tasks specific to viral infection. Although conventional software might occasionally contain one of these fragments, the presence of many of them is an almost certain viral hallmark. Anti-viral software can check for such short sequences very quickly; even more important, because these patterns of data are directly linked to the virus's function, we can now recognise a wide variety of viruses without ever having seen them before.

Just as external factors such as drought, sanitation and migration have a strong influence on biological epidemics, changes in the computing environment are responsible for the presence of several distinct epochs in viral infection. Until 1992, reported sightings of file-infecting viruses and boot viruses occurred at roughly equal (and steadily rising) rates. Then the incidence rate for file infectors began to fall dramatically, whereas that for boot-sector infectors continued to rise.

Between late 1992 and late 1995, boot-sector infectors reigned supreme. The cause is the widespread acceptance of Windows 3.1, an enhancement to MS-DOS—the operating system used on most computers—that became popular around 1992. Windows crashes readily in the presence of typical file viruses, and so necessity will lead afflicted users somehow to eliminate the virus from their systems, regardless of whether they know that the symptoms are caused by a virus. Boot viruses, in contrast, tend to coexist peacefully with Windows 3.1; they do not kill their hosts before the infection has a chance to run riot.

The wide use of Windows 95, yet another new operating system, has now led to a precipitous decline in the prevalence of boot viruses. Windows 95 warns the user about most changes to boot sectors, including many of those caused by viruses, and most boot viruses cannot spread under Windows 95.

Since users tend to exchange documents and other data files capable of harbouring macro viruses more frequently than they exchange programmes, macro viruses enjoy a higher birth rate and thus spread faster than the traditional boot or file infectors. Sophisticated mail and file-transfer functions now permit users to share documents or programmes more quickly and easily than before, exacerbating the problem. Macro viruses are also the first viruses to exploit the growing trend for interoperability among computers. A DOS file infector can never endanger a Macintosh, for instance, but a macro virus can infect any computer that supports a vulnerable application programme.

A successful new virus typically takes months or even years to gain a foothold. In the densely connected world of the near future, viruses might be able to propagate much faster. As early as 1988, Robert Tappan Morris launched what came to be known as the "internet worm", a programme that exploited security holes and invaded hundreds of computers around the world in less than a day. New technologies (such as web browsers that use "ActiveX") for silently downloading software and data to a user's computer make the problem even more pressing. Already modern-day mail programmes permit text documents or spreadsheets to be sent very simply as e-mail attachments. Opening the attachment can cause the appropriate application to start up automatically, and any macro viruses contained in the attachment may be executed. Soon software agents may be routinely authorised to send and open mail containing attachments. With humans no longer participating in the replication cycle, viruses could be free to spread orders of magnitude faster than they do now. These changes in the digital ecosystem suggest that a more automatic response to computer viruses is needed, one that is not limited by human response times or by the rate at which humans can dissect novel viruses.

IBM, Symantec Corporation and McAfee Associates are among the companies developing technology to help respond quickly and automatically to new viruses. The IBM is creating what may be thought of as an immune system for cyberspace. Just as the vertebrate immune system creates immune cells capable of fighting new pathogens within a few days of exposure, a computer immune system derives prescriptions for recognising and removing newly encountered computer viruses within minutes.

In a current prototype, PCs running IBM AntiVirus are connected by a network to a central computer that analyses viruses. A monitoring programme on each PC uses a variety of heuristics based on system behaviour, suspicious changes to programmes, or family signatures to infer that a virus may be present. The monitoring programme makes a copy of any programme thought to be infected and sends it over the network to the virus-analysis machine. On receiving a putatively infected sample, the machine sends it to another computer that acts as a digital petri dish. Software on this test machine lures the virus into infecting specially designed "decoy" programmes by executing, writing to, copying and otherwise manipulating the decoys. To replicate successfully, a virus must infect programmes that are used often, and so the decoy activity brings the viral code out of hiding.

Any decoys that have been infected can now be analysed by other components of the immune system, which will extract viral signatures and produce prescriptions for verifying and removing the virus. Typically it takes the virus analyser less than five minutes to produce such prescriptions from an infected sample. The analysis machine sends this information back to the infected client PC, which incorporates it into a permanent database of cures for known viruses. The PC is then directed to locate and remove all instances of the virus, and it is permanently protected from subsequent encounters. If the PC is connected to other machines on a local-area network, it is quite possible that the virus has invaded some of them as well.

CYBER THREATS: CHANGING SECURITY CONCEPTS

In the age of globalisation, post-Cold War politics, and daily information technology revolutions, national security interests have come to include human security, personal privacy, financial security, healthcare concerns, systemic educational concerns, and social ethics. National security concerns exist not only in the physical world, but also in the nebulous world of cyberspace. The triumph of market forces has combined with the spread of information technologies to create an entire 'new economy' where transactions are instantaneous and uninterrupted, and negotiations are often intangible or invisible. None the less, transactions occurring in this medium provide the fundamental basis for productivity and growth in every sector of human endeavour.

Thus it is important to distinguish different levels of national security, and to acknowledge the differences between the agencies of government involved directly in addressing national defence and those responsible for law enforcement, economic matters, or social policies. The severity of a cyber threat against a national military or critical infrastructure assets will require a very different response than a spate of criminal activity targeting financial institutions. In order to better understand and characterise the new threats to national security, a greater degree of transparency between the many parts of government addressing the problem is critical.

Advent of the information age also has created new national security roles for the public and private sectors, as well as new opportunities for the empowerment of individuals, small groups, and transnational non-state actors. As a result, threats no longer originate simply from armies or national entities. At the same time, the ownership and responsibility for maintenance and protection of national infrastructure assets such as roads and airspace, and tightly knit assets such as telephone and electrical power distribution, are more widely diversified than was the case with wholly owned government assets. The fact that infrastructure ownership continues to evolve as rapidly as infrastructure dependence presents substantial new challenges for all governments, and these are compounded by the increasing number of assets requiring government protection.

There are several recent examples of how formerly industry-specific concerns have risen—or have the potential to rise—to the level of national security concerns. Perhaps the most recent example is the admission by Microsoft that hackers had broken into their systems and accessed next-generation Windows software that was not only unreleased, but not yet even announced. A profound concern to both private and public entities becomes whether or not any of these products will be trustworthy once they are released. More troubling still is the admission that the hackers used a relatively unsophisticated programme (the QAZ Trojan Horse) to penetrate the security perimeter of the world's most powerful software company. With most military and government systems powered by Microsoft software and more generally reliant on COTS, this recent development can pose grave security-related concerns.

However till today, no severe incidents of nation-based cyber-warfare have been detected. At the level of smaller actors, however, the statistics are much more telling. According to interpol, 30,000 hacker websites currently exist on the internet. In the ten years between 1989 and 1999, there were only 34,000 reported global hacking incidents in aggregate, but between January and October 2000 alone, 50,000 incidents were reported.

In 1999, 22,144 attacks against unclassified US military computer systems were detected by the Department of Defence (DoD). It is difficult to estimate the financial repercussions of such a volume of attacks on a global scale. Studies undertaken to date, however, point to disconcerting figures, many of which are all the more alarming because they represent conservative estimates. As the figures grow, they begin to rival statistics for bricks-and-mortar crimes such as check fraud and offline credit card fraud, currently the two most significant sources of loss at financial institutions.

Although the direct destructive effects of cyber threats are on a lesser scale, they can have severe impacts on national objectives and security interests. Since the profound interconnectivities and interdependencies created by the internet, attacks can easily be multiplied, copied, or modified. The focus of the attackers is not merely on perceptions or targets, but on security goals. Disrupting national objectives does not require as much time or as many actors as it once did. The impacts are not only more complex, but also more pervasive. The destruction of an individual target is a tragedy; the destruction of targets in aggregate—be they embassies, dams, or power grids—becomes a direct threat to national security. There is a low probability of a single point of failure. Of greater concern are coordinated and repeated multiple points of failure that can cause significant disruption. The multiplication effect empowered by the internet can cause what would normally be considered a tactical attack to escalate rapidly to the level of the strategic. Lines of defence and accountability often lie in the hands of individuals and smaller organisations.

Threats emanating from the convergence of multiple technologies and sciences present tremendous potential for severe damage and disruption to critical infrastructures and national assets, but are poorly understood by those responsible for their prevention. While many experts contend that serious threats—the kind that would perpetuate damage on the scale of conventional attacks—will not manifest themselves on the immediate horizon, there is nonetheless an urgent imperative to focus on concrete preventive measures. When viruses that are more sophisticated and malicious than those sustained in recent months, there will be little time for rational analysis and preparation.

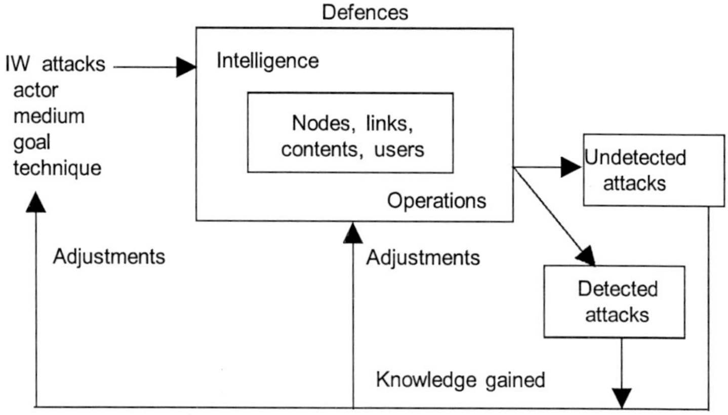

Figure 6.2: Threat dynamics

Setting up preventive measures and contingency plans is challenging, particularly as the effects and potential impacts of information attacks are still being evaluated. The effects of a missile attack are known and the damage is quantifiable.

However, forecasting the damage wrought by the stealing of information, interruption of service, and destruction of data is very different from the well-established methodologies designed to assess damage from conventional attacks. Until "real" cyber incidents occur, i.e., those inflicting physical, emotional, or economic loss on the scale of conventional attacks, it will be difficult to predict the true damage caused by such attacks, or the success of proposed attacks.

Compounding the challenge of anticipating and planning for threats to national infrastructures is the issue of the attacker's motivation. While some cyber attacks are indeed national security threats, others merely emanate from cyber thrill-seekers. The May 2000 "Love Bug", unleashed by two junior college dropouts in the Philippines, caused several billion dollars in lost business and information, and permanently damaged files and data. However, the underlying motivation was not economic gain but braggadocio that had political repercussions. Several sorts of threats emerge from this new environment, each with varying levels of national security concern:

i) The threat of disruption of communication flows, economic transactions, public information campaigns, electrical power grids, political negotiations, water distribution, and other components of the national infrastructure. The effects of disruptions usually will be felt purely in economic terms, and thus will be of greatest concern to private sector entities. However, the disruption of military communications in times of conflict presents the potential for loss of life or aborted military missions. The probability of this type of threat materialising is considerable, as the tools required to create disruptive viruses and denial-of-service attacks are already pervasive and constantly being improved.

ii) The threat of exploitation of sensitive, proprietary, or classified information. Information theft, fraud, and cybercrime can have serious effects. From identity theft to online credit card fraud to the systemic probing of government systems, exploitation can have an impact on anyone. The threat is made all the more ominous by the difficulty in detecting these types of intrusions and compromised systems. As with disruption, the probability of occurrence is high and there have been several notable examples in recent months. These types of attacks most often are sporadic, isolated, and motivated by personal financial gain or by the desire to expose certain systems as insecure. However, exploitation also can be systematic and state-sponsored. For example, an ongoing series of structured, persistent, purposeful probes into university, government, and private sector systems in the United States, allegedly originating in Russia, was detected in 1999. This operation —codenamed Moonlight Maze—was ongoing for a year before being detected. While the systems themselves have not been damaged, the attackers have stolen considerable amounts of unclassified but sensitive information. The attacks that continued through 2000 emanated from different parts of the Former Soviet Republics. Moscow has denied any involvement. The attacks have not been disruptive, but are dangerous in aggregate.

iii) The threat of manipulation of information for political, economic or military purposes, or for bragging rights. Several recent incidents of defaced websites in the former Yugoslavia and the Middle East, and of altered personal financial information on e-commerce sites, point to the clear potential for using the internet as a powerful tool for information manipulation. This manipulation also can occur in combination with disruption or exploitation. In a recent attack, the pro-Palestinian "Pakistani Hackerz Club" not only defaced the website of the American Israel Public Affairs Committee, they also downloaded 3,500 e-mail addresses to which they sent anti-Israeli messages, and 700 credit card numbers of members who had made donations to the organisation, which they promptly published on the internet. While many instances of manipulation simply serve the cause of making a statement, and can be remedied rapidly, the more dangerous instances are those that go undetected: manipulation of financial data, military information, health-care information, or infrastructure data.

iv) The threat of destruction of information or its underpinning infrastructure components can have deleterious consequences for the economy and national security. Sophisticated attacks against highly specific power distribution and fuel manufacturing infrastructure targets in Serbia demonstrated the efficacy of such attacks. Destruction of information is of particular concern because it can be carried out through relatively simple hacker techniques. Examples are well documented. "The Love Bug" not only clogged e-mail boxes and stole passwords, it also caused files to be deleted from hard drives. The probability of major destruction of infrastructure remains low due to better security precautions surrounding critical national assets.

Globalisation and the advent of the information age have empowered individuals, national subgroups, and non-state actors. Since the internet is so pervasive and because hacker tools are increasingly cheap, accessible, and easy to weaponise, threats come not only from other nation-states, but from national opposition groups, ideological radicals, terrorist organisations, and individuals. Thus, both the likely criminal entities and the damage they seek to inflict become more difficult to identify, quantify, and warn against.

It is increasingly complicated to distinguish between a national security threat, criminal activity, and malicious but low-level disruption. In addition, globalisation has made it difficult for government to focus its actions on threats to international networks, as the government structure has not kept pace with the new transnational environment. Compounding the challenge is the fact that basic security practices and technologies are underutilised in both the public and private sectors. There is no silver bullet solution to addressing the societal and security threats that will continue to grow as information technologies become increasingly sophisticated and transparent. At the heart of the challenge lies the lack of alignment between authority, responsibility, and capability between the public and private sectors. Under current government structures and public-private partnerships, those with the authority to act often lack the capability, while those with the capability (and understanding) do not necessarily have a responsibility (or jurisdiction) to act. Aligning these dimensions of the public-private problem is critical to a nation's ability to counter cyber threats.

Several straightforward measures given below can be taken to improve security features and practices to protect individual businesses and agencies as well as critical national assets.

i) Encouraging increased reciprocal information-sharing with the private sector concerning vulnerabilities and solutions, particularly with respect to shared systems.

ii) Providing private sector industries with incentives for improving their security practices beyond the bare minimum demanded by market pressures and profit concerns. These incentives range from tax breaks to relief from specific provisions of antitrust laws to the clear establishment of corporate liability, liability limits, and extraordinary liability relief provisions, with attendant insurance measures.

iii) Promoting and requiring dramatic improvement in internal government practices, from consistent use of basic anti-virus software to greater education and training of security professionals to personal accountability for sensitive information. Measures must also include improved interagency information-sharing and a conscious, sophisticated public information and education campaign.

iv) Moving away from the current passive response posture to a culture of planned, strategic response that will both provide the necessary preparedness and authority for agencies to act effectively in the event of a cyber attack, and ensure the capacity not only for defence but also for retribution.

v) Establishing and adjusting the legal infrastructure required to support the prevention, remediation, or prosecution of cyber crimes, acts of cyberterrorism, or acts of information warfare, both at the domestic and at the international level.

Addressing cyber threats is gradually becoming a more central facet of defence concerns and strategies. Attacks from nation-states are difficult to distinguish from those launched by non-state actors, who in turn are hard to identify, hedge against, or apprehend. For example, transnational pseudo-religious groups are evolving with a more sophisticated generation of IT users from physical to electronic terrorism. A national security strategy addressing cyber concerns also must focus on domestic threats, as "insiders" remain the leading perpetrators of all cyber incidents.

As incidents of cyber disruption, crime, and manipulation increase both in numbers and in visibility, and stated vulnerabilities are proven, the tradeoffs between improving protection and preserving efficiency will undoubtedly be reevaluated, both on a corporate and on a societal level. At the heart of the information security conundrum is the prevalence of behavioral problems endemic to the information age—even where good security procedures are in place in government and private organisations, they often are ignored or violated because they are too complex or cumbersome.

Government staff and company employees operate under extreme time pressures, and their top priority is to meet their responsibilities at any cost. For example, they might do classified work on a laptop while at home or travelling. The challenge of ensuring proper remote handling of sensitive or classified data will be compounded by a recent government initiative to encourage telecommuting. The issues of security and accountability have not been thought through by the agencies monitoring the trend toward work outside the office. A recent example of damage caused by sheer human neglect is the case of Western Union, USA, where a worker performing system maintenance inadvertently left the firewall open. Some 15,700 accounts were compromised as a result, and the damage to Western Union's formerly solid reputation in the marketplace was considerable. Many recent instances of stolen credit card numbers or compromised personal data are due to the inadequate use of firewalls or to the lack of personal precautions with "always-on" home connections via DSL. These technologies and remedies are simple and cost-effective. The central problem is a lack of education and awareness. For the average consumer, ease of use currently takes precedence over security, and software therefore is designed with only those security features that will allow its use to be less cumbersome to the consumer. Thus, sophisticated encryption and multiple layers of firewalls are shunned for speed, accessibility of data, and minimal password memorisation.

With information technologies becoming increasingly small, cheap, fast, and ubiquitous, national infrastructures and critical domestic assets are undergoing rapid and inevitable internationalisation. The growing co-dependence of public and private organisations on common systems, networks, and COTS hardware and software is shifting the ownership of these infrastructures and assets into the hands of those with the most efficient research, development, and production. While the private sector progresses rapidly and independently with new software development, and often with international corporate collaboration, the bureaucratic procedures embedded in the public sectors of most national governments prevent them from keeping pace.

As groups working across regions and borders clamour for shrink-wrapped, standardised products, the lack of "biological diversity" in existing software packages and the emergence of open source software create profound security loopholes. International collaboration and outsourcing of research and management, software development, and coding for common operating systems compound the difficulty for both private and especially public entities to place boundaries on their systems and networks. National borders are not lines on the map of information infrastructure, because ownership of and responsibility for the network becomes increasingly diverse as the level of detail increases. On a general level, the major pieces of the infrastructure can be said to be owned by a few large telecommunications providers in the private sector or as entities in partially socialised economies.

Incidents that were once locally confined now can have international repercussions, and cross both public and private lines. Actual IW and cyberwar are still difficult to carry out on a large scale. However, IW strategies are increasingly becoming embedded in national defence plans and intelligence operations of countries all over the world. Although many experts believe that the threat from nation-states is currently overstated, the potential for sophisticated cyberwar tactics is likely to evolve rapidly. In addition, intelligence-gathering on information attacks poses strong challenges legally and operationally.

Although no serious nation-based attacks have been detected to date, it is important to note that many documented attacks have had national organisations behind them, or have supported nationalist motives. In contrast to the still nebulous threat from nation-states, the threat from subgroups and terrorist organisations is very real. While their goal is neither war nor destruction on a large scale, the effects of attacks from politically motivated groups are likely to be more pervasive. Their goal scan be disruption, intimidation, or publication of a political message, as many previously discussed examples illustrate.

Accuracy and scale are less important to nationally motivated hackers than general disruption. Few cyber incidents to date have qualified as "terrorist", as measured in the conventional sense. Most incidents have been criminal ones, or acts of cyber thrill-seeking, denial-of-service, and virus release. While loss of life is not a concern with these sorts of attacks, the damage has generally been quantifiable in dollar amounts that command respect and deserve attention. The cost of lost information, interrupted operations, damage to documents, server cleanups, overtime for IT employees, and the like, quickly adds up. For example, losses from the "Love Bug" worm alone have been estimated as high as eight billion dollars. The disruptive Melissa virus, although not damaging to files and systems, none the less caused many companies to shut down their e-mail systems to disinfect them.

The internationalisation of the internet has made it an important medium for coalescing disparate groups into common action—on a permanent or temporary basis—around one or more issues, with profound international repercussions. The impacts of the disruptions at the 1999 World Trade Organisation (WTO) Ministerial Conference in Seattle, spurred by interest groups and non-governmental organisations uniting online, are once again not quantifiable in conventional terms, but are significant. The activists overcame national and international objectives to push their anti-capitalist global agenda. Subsequently, although with lesser effects, they rallied to disrupt meetings in Washington, D.C., and World Bank and International Monetary Fund (IMF) meetings in Prague. The momentum achieved in assailing the negotiations in Seattle arguably could not have been achieved without the enabling medium of the internet. Many have credited the internet with the resonant political success of other grassroots movements such as the campaign that led to the International Treaty to Ban Landmines.

National governments have been slow to react to cyber vulnerabilities, even when faced with the evidence. There are many reasons for this. On the personnel side, there is a shortage of technical experts, a lack of adequate training for non-technical employees using information systems to handle sensitive information, and insufficient employee background checks to hedge against insider threats. The intelligence community, while enforcing stricter information management rules due to the classified nature of much of its data, finds itself with similar limitations with respect to technically skilled analysts. Moreover, the community is extremely fragmented organisationally and is risk averse when it comes to addressing cyber issues.

Law enforcement agencies are under-funded and under-staffed, and have shown themselves to be limited in their information-sharing and dissemination due to the importance of their own information protection mission. Their focus on successful prosecution comes at the expense of a much-needed emphasis on prevention. Pervasive social concerns about privacy have also preoccupied government, at a time when private information is more exposed than it ever has been, and the balance between privacy and public safety—which are complementary, not mutually exclusive—is constantly being renegotiated.

While the problems of infrastructure protection and cyber threats can be countered to some degree on a national level, a global perspective clearly is required for an effective overall response.

The private sector owns most of the infrastructure but remains sceptical about the seriousness of the vulnerabilities, and the government has done very little to make the case that larger threats to the infrastructure exist. None the less, both government organisations and private corporations have taken steps to fulfil their obligations, and those capabilities should be looked at for their intentions, their results, and their potential effectiveness in addressing known and presumed threats.

In the case of cyber threats, a definition of national information infrastructure assets is a crucial starting point. The governments's obligation should include all aspects, physical and informational, of defending and ensuring the functional reliability of any non-nodal segment of the global network. It should encompass, to varying degrees, the defence of networks and systems which are necessary for the continuation of government, for the continuing efficacy of armed forces, for the continued growth and stability of the economy, and for the safety of the public. In all of these cases, this responsibility applies to threats both foreign and domestic, from any level of actor ranging from individual on up to nation-state, and whether criminal, political, or military in intent. Governments also must stipulate clear provisions for countering or punishing attacks.

Since so much of the critical value and ownership of the infrastructure lies in private hands, the private sector plays a significant and often uncomfortable role in information infrastructure protection. Businesses, institutions, and corporations all increasingly depend on the internet for both commercial and personal transactions. The security of the information infrastructure therefore is becoming as critical to their success, solvency, and continuity of operations as the protection of telephone, power, or transportation systems. Many companies recognised their dependencies early on, as well as their need for appropriate security measures. These corporations—in particular financial institutions, utilities groups, and software companies—not only have undertaken internal precautionary measures, many are starting to publicly convey a message of increased protection. By contrast, other often smaller companies appear blissfully unaware of the threat, or choose not to expend the personnel and resources necessary to protect themselves.

According to a 1999 study by the Gartner Group, Inc., in US most companies spend less than 1 per cent of their operating budgets on information security, and few see a compelling reason to spend more. The private sector's obligation with respect to protecting the national information infrastructure is uniquely different from other infrastructure-related national security concerns. However, it is conceptually harder for organisations and individuals to grasp the value of less tangible assets such as information and access, and therefore, security measures taken in the virtual world do not parallel those taken for granted in the physical world. Underestimating the costs of a failure in information infrastructure is probably the deciding factor in ensuring the low level of interest in the subject on the part of the private sector. This is due to some extent to the sheer difficulty of estimating the cost of damages, and the widely varying estimates used in the media do little to lend weight to the potential threat. Commercial organisations, as well as government agencies, are still learning to take advantage of the opportunities that present themselves in a networked environment. As such, they have not yet reacted effectively to use the available capabilities to effectively protect themselves, nor have the recognised the business-case importance of doing their part to protect information infrastructure.

Effective information sharing is one of the most critical aspects to effective information infrastructure protection, and could be an area in which the private sector truly excels. However, no particular industry or trade either owns or is disproportionately dependent on the information infrastructure, leaving a leadership void in the cause of spreading awareness of problems, threats, and solutions. Commercial organisations generally rely on government to provide the means of communication when the distribution channels are diverse and scattered.

Since it has access to data identifying vulnerabilities and ongoing threats, the government is in a unique position—and has a unique obligation—to provide the public with the motivation it requires to undertake the protective measures that the marketplace has neglected. Unfortunately, when addressing private entities, the government generally has employed histrionic national security arguments rather than stating their case based on more tangible economic factors.

Improved and enhanced mechanisms for information sharing will be the crucial first step in any government initiative to convince the private sector that it needs to do more to hedge against cyber threats. Information sharing must be part of a larger government strategy, wherein communications take place not only between government and the private sector but between different government agencies, particularly between the national security and law enforcement communities. "Information sharing" is a broad and complex concept; however, certain forms of information are more crucial in improving the prevention of cyber incidents, and also are more readily shared among groups and institutions. The critical types of information that government and industry should exchange are the following:

i) *Known network vulnerabilities:* If a company or government agency has carried out an assessment of its own networks and generated data, it can act to secure its systems more effectively, and can share the nature of some of its former vulnerabilities with others, to save them both time and risk. A barrier to this type of sharing emerges when there are legal concerns over due diligence

ii) *Warning of ongoing attacks or threats, without "sources and methods" attribution:* The individuals likely to first detect intrusions or attacks are system administrators and network administrators. They are reluctant to report these intrusions to law enforcement, as they fear that proprietary information will be compromised, or their corporate reputation will suffer if the intrusions are made public. When ongoing attacks are reported, law enforcement should find ways of sanitising the information, analysing it, and disseminating it among the organisations that also could be affected, thus identifying potential vulnerabilities or attacks without naming the institution or company under attack. This information-sharing by law enforcement is particularly crucial in the case of systematic attacks or probes that are known to law enforcement because they are pervasive enough to be a national security concern, or because they originate in a specific foreign nation.

iii) *Strategies for defending against certain types of attack:* When an individual institution locates a vulnerability or is made aware of one, and finds a solution, it resists sharing that information because of the proprietary value of its solution. Again, the government function should be to sanitise and disseminate the information in a way that supports prevention for other companies but does not reveal the identity of the company providing the solution. Companies could be asked to provide information on new viruses, or on the apparent *modus operandi* of a given attacker, or on information gleaned from meetings with hackers who have identified specific targets for attack. This will help establish and identify signatures and improve sensors for better future protection.

Due to recent negative trends in information sharing, and to provide an added incentive to the private sector, government must show that it is willing to initiate the dialogue, to "share first". Effective cooperation will flow from capitalisation on comparative advantages. The government has the core insights on critical infrastructure protection from a national security perspective. The private sector, on the other hand, has the core insights on information security management.

Risk in cyber attacks is difficult to quantify because of the lack of experience and actuarially based data. As deaths currently are unlikely to result from hacking, the end-state is not likely to be as dramatic as it has been in other industries that have galvanised insurance and litigation processes. Governments should be the catalyst for the establishment of parameters and standards, but not the enforcer. Industry should participate in establishing standards on a voluntary basis, based on their superior understanding of and investment in the various facets of information technology. Some pragmatic suggestions of incentives that the governments can provide to the private sector above and beyond information-sharing include:

i) Tax breaks or equivalent "credits" can be established for companies that utilise certified safety products that have been inspected by an accredited organisation, and that strictly enforce certain types of security procedures and behaviours.

ii) The governments should further invest or co-invest in new technologies and in its own internal research and developments. Public endorsement also should be provided clearly to companies that manufacture safety products or that expand their products' range.

iii) The government should facilitate a private sector dialogue and consensus-based mechanism for certifying the safety and effectiveness of security products on the marketplace.

iv) Insurance companies should be encouraged to include limited liability indemnification insurance policies against cyber disruption in their insurance portfolios. They should join forces with security technology companies to establish basic requirements for coverage, and government can once again provide the role of facilitator. Insurers could require that minimum standards be met, and might underwrite the establishment of organisations to set those standards. The top information security firms already have checklists for companies to use in evaluating their security practices.

v) Liability limits against disruption of service can be established if a company utilises certified products and meets established "best practices". These practices would be evaluated based on annual (or biannual) inspections. The inspections are critical as certified components are not sufficient in and of themselves for prevention. The design of the overall system, the implementation and configuration of the design, the maintenance and upkeep of the configuration, the provision of measures for physical security and personnel security, are all necessary as well. In addition, careful consideration should be given to a proposal to grant relief from antitrust laws to like-minded corporations that share information and collaborate purely in matters of information security.

vi) Clear corporate liability should be established in order to transfer risk from the shoulders of consumers onto companies providing software or services. Most companies have become very dependent on the internet, and many are wide open to significant liabilities they are not paying much attention to. This risk transfer would encourage companies both to purchase insurance and to improve their fraud detection or intrusion detection systems. This process has proven highly successful with the credit card industry.

vii) Personal liability and accountability should be encouraged not only within government but also for the CIOs, CEOs, and boards of directors that govern private corporations. Establishing clear lines of responsibility will serve to encourage more stringent security measures and practices within companies.

viii) Extraordinary liability relief should be provided in the case of cyberwarfare, similar to indemnification authorities for destruction of commercial assets through conventional warfare. In addition, financial relief for digital "disasters" akin to natural disasters should be given careful consideration. In the latter case, insurance executives have suggested that the government should be the "insurer of last resort". Insurance companies would insure up to a certain level, which remains to be determined; a consortium of insurance, software, and hardware companies could create a pool for reinsurance purposes; and the government would intervene in cases of massive outages or shutdowns.

ix) Intermediate regulatory steps should be suggested for systems that are common to public and private entities.

> There are several precedents for the domestic and international regulation of shared systems, for example, in air and sea transport policies, or in the control of infectious diseases. As with the issue of mandates, the problem of quantifying risk is important—infectious diseases lead to significant casualties, while cyber incidents have not.

The governments have to articulate a commonly agreed-upon, clearly defined position on what it considers an information attack, and on how and under what conditions it will respond. Without this fundamental policy premise, it is very difficult to formulate event sequence scenarios that would necessitate planning, defence, and response. This in turn complicates the task of devising viable forms of timely and effective reaction or retaliation, as well as realistic offensive Information Warfare (IW) and Information Operations (IO) capabilities. National information infrastructure protection must be viewed as an ongoing concern, rather than as a series of disjointed incidents of varying magnitudes.

One of the challenges faced by governments in providing motivation to the private sector is not only its poor articulation of the problem, but also its abysmal track record of leadership by example. An ideal starting point lies in the more effective protection of government systems, including simple measures such as installing virus-protection software upgrades and patches in a timely manner. In addition to demonstrating competence by establishing more effective protection of its own systems, government can provide incentives such as procurement and grant programmes to encourage the same level of information systems and network protection in academia and in state and local governments.

Expansion in the global use of information weapons for troublemaking, political, or criminal purposes has created a significant noise floor of spurious incidents, which can shroud serious hostile activities such as espionage, intelligence collection, and state-sponsored network mapping or information attacks. This haze—referred to in more conventional terms as the "fog of war"—makes it increasingly difficult for the government to discern legitimate national security threats from the acts of common criminals or thrill-seeking hackers.

While rapid identification of perpetrators remains a challenge, it must be noted that the technical capabilities for remediation, tactical response, and investigation (trap-and-trace) increase in sophistication on a daily basis. Fog of war problems can be addressed on a technical level by investing real resources into tracking the flow of information through packet switching routing networks like the internet. The obstacles to an effective response to information attacks remain primarily in the realms of policy, mindset, and personnel, particularly in law enforcement and intelligence.

The response against information attacks must be part of a broad and clearly articulated national response plan, ensuring the capability to respond immediately to an attack, or to counter a known threat, irrespective of its origin—be it domestic, international, national, or subnational in nature. Additionally, a serious analytic cadre should be built and maintained to support investigations and activities on an ongoing basis.

A critical element of adopting a comprehensive, active response policy is to greatly increase the speed of response to cyber incidents, particularly those with potentially cascading effects throughout the infrastructure. Unlike "conventional" forms of warfare or terrorism, preparations for and the initiation of cyber attacks are not easily perceived. The anonymity of the internet lends itself well to the covert and invisible launching of coordinated attacks, using the low-level noise mentioned previously as cover. Planning a three month window to address hostile activities that may last for only seconds or minutes, and for which varying degrees of immediate response must be available both for deterrence of further attacks and retribution against existing ones, is not a viable policy by any standard.

Basic mechanisms for identifying and countering insider threats are necessary, particularly as the government is actually relaxing personal security requirements in many areas. At the core of solutions within the public sector is the need for vastly improved education and training. This includes promoting awareness of security issues as a central component of all government business; the encouragement of technical competency through continuing education and access to cutting-edge courses; personnel incentives for promotion and growth; a re-evaluation of key retention factors such as competitive salaries and healthcare or other benefits; and a substantial increase in the number of cyber professionals through recruitment directly from undergraduate or graduate programmes and through incentives to educational institutions.

Successful models already exist within specific sectors. For example, in US, the National Cybercrime Training Partnership (NCTP) works across agencies to provide multi-level, geographically decentralised, and dynamic training to law enforcement agencies and officials at the federal, state, and local levels, in responding to electronic and high technology crime. Another example is the "Cyber Corps" of computer experts, which has received continued funding for the coming fiscal year. These efforts represent a noble beginning, but must be supplemented with mission-specific training for computer scientists and engineers hired into government service. This training must focus on building multiple competencies, to include a real military offensive network warfare capability, "cyber" counter-intelligence analysts and operatives, human factors analysts who can ascertain motivations, and a competent public relations staff to effectively educate the public on the vulnerabilities of individual and networked PCs.

Education will be critical to promoting the appropriate societal context for improvements in security-related behaviours in both private and public realms, and policies will need to be established to encourage the development of educational programmes at all levels. The shortage of qualified information security experts points not only to the need to train security professionals on the job, but also to the need for improvement of computer science or MIS education, where security and reliability of systems have not been important design considerations.

Government encouragement of and incentives for university funding for information security programmes and faculty is essential. Recent initiatives have provided a positive step toward this goal. For example, in US on October 27, 2000, President Bill Clinton announced a "Scholarship for Service" programme that will provide up to two years of scholarship funding for students studying information security, in return for a commitment to work for an equal amount of time for the federal government. This initiative is one of five education and training programmes stipulated under the National Plan, and will be administered by the National Science Foundation (NSF).

Investigations and prosecutions of computer crime fly in the face of national sovereignty and jurisdictional issues. With roughly 210 countries on the internet, individual sets of bilateral agreements would not be bureaucratically feasible. Therefore, common international platforms must be achieved. The primary goals of any international agreement should be to:

i) Clearly define what constitutes a hostile act, namely, where to draw the lines between attack and annoyance.

ii) Clearly define what actions are required for a legal response, including whether a target must be notified before retribution is exacted, and if so, under what circumstances.

iii) Include language to facilitate working around technical problems and limitations. In particular, this language should allow for a response policy that does not require certainty of the identity or even nature of the source of the attack.

iv) Require cooperation, within acceptable limits, in addressing attribution of attacks, and subsequent potential retribution, in order not to compromise the national interests of a country that is merely a way point in an attack.

Many countries already have very specific definitions and laws in place concerning cyber crimes. These laws can help deter, prosecute, and occasionally sentence perpetrators. They also can help establish a common international definition of cyber crimes, paving the way for more coherent international policies.

Agreements between nations will of necessity stretch beyond the issues of crime, terrorism, or warfare. Recently, French courts have raised a significant and compelling argument that has spurred debate on transnational regulation of the internet. The French courts have asked Yahoo! Inc., to block French viewers from visiting areas of its auction sites that sell Nazi memorabilia. Although Yahoo! is a US-based company and this request runs against US free speech principles, it is validated by French anti-racist and anti-hate-crime laws which prohibit the sale of such artifacts in France. The court decision treads on the uncharted territory of enforcing national laws upon global online services. France has set an interesting precedent for zoning and regulation of the internet, and for providing courts with the authority to impose sanctions outside of their normal jurisdictions. Cases such as these stress the pressing need for clear, agreed-upon international standards governing jurisdictional issues. In establishing international conventions and treaties, it would be useful to examine existing models for international collaboration based on safety concerns.

REFERENCES

Borchgrave, Arnaud de, et al., "Cyber Threats and Information Security: Meeting the 21st Century Challenge", Center for

Strategic and International Studies, Washington, D.C., December 2000.

Cheswick, W. R., and S. M. Bellovin, *Firewalls and Internet Security: Repelling the Wily Hacker,* Addison-Wesley, 1994.

Denning, Dorothy E., and William E. Baugh, Jr., *Encryption and Evolving Technologies As Tools of Organized Crime and Terrorism,* Washington, D.C.: U.S. Working Group on Organized Crime (WGOC), National Strategy Information Center, 1997.

Edward, Taylor, B., "Building a Minefield Database System", *Engineer* 26, pp.14-16, December 1996.

Hansen, M. H., *Modern Methods for Computer Security and Privacy*, Prentice-Hall, 1977.

Hatch, Brian, James Lee, George Kurtz, *Hacking Linux Exposed: Linux Security Secrets and Solutions*, McGraw-Hill Professional Book Group, April 2001.

Howard, John D., *An Analysis of Internet Security Incidents, 1989–1995.* unpublished dissertation., Pittsburgh, Penn.: Carnegie Mellon University, 1997.

Hundley, Richard O., and Robert H. Anderson, "Emerging Challenge: Security and Safety in Cyberspace", *IEEE Technology and Society Magazine,* Vol. 14, No. 4, pp. 19–28, Winter 1995–1996.

Northcutt, Stephen, Judy Novak, Donald McLachlan, *Network Intrusion Detection: An Analyst's Handbook*, New Riders Publishing, September 2000.

Paige, Emmett, Jr., "The Future of Information Security", *Defense Issues* 11, no. 71, pp.1-3, 1996.

Parker, Donna, *Fighting Computer Crime: A New Framework for Protecting Information*, Wiley, John & Sons, Incorporated, August 1998.

Potter, David L., "Information Warfare: Malicious Software and Technology", *Military Intelligence* 23, pp.34-37, January-March 1997.

Robert Slade, *Robert Slade's GuideTo Computer Viruses: How to Avoid Them, How To Get Rid Of Them And How To Get Help*, Springer-Verlag New York, Incorporated, March 1996.

Rosenblatt, K. S., *High Technology Crime: Investigating Cases Involving Computers*, KSK Publications, San Jose, CA, 1995.

Schmauder, Phil, *Virus Proof: The Ultimate Guide to Protecting Your System with CD-ROM*, Prima Communications, Inc., April 2000.

Schwartzstein, Stuart J.D., (ed.), *The Information Revolution and National Security: Dimensions and Directions*, Washington: Center for Strategic and International Studies, 1996.

Skardhamar, Rune, *Virus: Detection and Elimination*, Academic Press, Incorporated, October 1995.

Stallings, William, *Network Security Essentials: Applications and Standards*, Prentice Hall PTR, November 1999.

Toxen, Bob, *Real World Linux Security: Intrusion Prevention, Detection and Recovery with CD-ROM*, Prentice Hall PTR, November 2000.

Wilson, E., "The Information Revolution and National Security", Draft, Center for International Development and Conflict Management, College Park, Md.: University of Maryland, October 31, 1995.

7

Ethical Issues

The development of information technology, specifically computers, telecommunications, and networks, makes it possible for adversaries to attack each other in new ways and with new forms of damage, and may create new targets for attack. Attackers may use international networks to damage or disrupt enemy systems, without ever physically entering the enemy's country, and countries' dependence upon electronic or other information-based systems may make those systems particularly attractive targets. Furthermore, the dual-use nature of many information systems and infrastructures may blur the distinction between military and civilian targets.

The weapons of information warfare (IW) have effects as potentially devastating as those of nuclear weapons, yet there has been relatively little closure in the debates on the implications of the newest technologies and their use in warfare. The use of technology designed to destroy or incapacitate an enemy's communications or information infrastructure will fall, during hostilities, under the auspices of the Law of Armed Conflict. The two principles by which any act of aggression must be measured under these laws are necessity and proportionality. An attack must be necessary for a military purpose, and the damage it causes must be worth the advantage that is gained. It is under these rules that global thermonuclear warfare became obsolete.

One basic tenet of international law is that attacks against civilians are prohibited. In the passage referred to previously, the author considers attacks on a country's airline reservation system. The operational commander would have a difficult time justifying this action under the test of military necessity. Attacks against a country's financial, transportation, or communications systems must be shown to have clear military necessity to be legal. Even in the more mundane forms of IW, such as destruction of an enemy's command and control capability, law of armed conflict questions may restrict the operational commander. In Operation Desert Storm, coalition air forces targeted radio stations, telephone exchanges, and microwave stations. From a purely legal standpoint, intelligence will have to provide evidence that targets like these are being used by the military to be considered as legal targets.

One can imagine a perfectly executed command and control warfare attack that leaves the enemy leadership with no means to communicate with his forces. There are several reasons, however, why this might not be the ideal situation for the commander. The first is the most obvious. Should the perfect IW campaign leave the enemy command with no means to fight, it is then none the less unable to communicate its desire for surrender or truce to its troops. Military units are trained to fight autonomously in the event of lost communications, and, until a reliable and believable command to halt hostilities is received from superiors, they are likely to continue the struggle.

Another consideration is the link between an enemy's information flow and the commander's attempts at military deception. While deception may be aided by degraded communications, severely deteriorated information flow may instead negate attempts at military deception. Often the desired end of a deception plan is not simply to prevent the enemy from gaining knowledge of an operation, but in fact to cause him to distribute his forces unwisely, and to his disadvantage.

ETHICAL ISSUES OF IW

From the dawn of the recorded history of conflict, attempts have been made to craft an ethical approach to war. They break down into two categories: a set of guidelines regarding going to war at all and a set of strictures by which combatants, should they adhere to them, might fight during a war in a just manner. These dimensions of the ethical approach to war have received searching scrutiny. In this early period of the information age, the time has come to revisit these ethical concepts, as new forms of conflict are emerging to test existing understanding of 'just wars'—much as advanced information technologies are already requiring a rethinking of a wide range of commercial and criminal laws. IW is a concept that ranges from the use of cyberspace to attack communication nodes and infrastructures to the use of information media in the service of psychological influence techniques. Since it constitutes such a variety of conflict modes, IW poses problems for those who seek out ethical guidelines for its waging.

Concepts of Just War Theory

From ancient to modern times, a remarkable consistency characterises thinking about just wars. Thus, nearly three millennia ago, concerns were advanced about the need for an ethical approach to going to war, as well as to waging war. The key concepts of the age old just war theory fall into the categories of criteria for going to war *(jus ad bellum)* and fighting justly during war *(jus in bello)*:

Tenets of Just War (Jus ad Bellum)

i) *Right purpose*: Justifiable reasons for going to war revolve around the concept of self-defence. Notions of right purpose generally include such ideas as pre-emption (i.e., striking in anticipation of an oncoming attack), but are less open to the idea that preventive war (i.e., striking at a propitious time) is just. Also, this category excludes wars of conquest or annexation.

ii) *Duly constituted authority*: It is clear from all the literature on ethics and war that a necessary condition for having a just war is that the decision to fight must come from a government—not from an individual. Wars waged by individuals have always fallen outside the law, the best example being provided by nineteenth-century prohibitions on the practice of private wars, or "filibusters", as they were then known.

iii) *Last resort*: Simply put, war cannot be considered just unless it follows exhaustive pursuit of negotiations and other means of conflict resolution.

Concepts of Just Warfighting (Jus in Bello)

iv) *Non-combatant immunity*: Wherever and whenever possible, according to just war theory, those waging the war must strive to avoid harming civilians or enemy troops that have surrendered. Fleeing troops that have no ability to fight fall into a gray area ethically, attacks upon them being allowed—but not encouraged. Conventional aerial bombing and, later, nuclear war, have posed problems for the notion of non-combatant immunity that remain unresolved. One attempt to cope with this was by considering air and nuclear attacks on strategic targets as permissible, with civilian losses treated as "collateral".

v) *Proportionality*: There are several aspects to this notion. First, and best known, is the issue of using force in a manner avoiding excessive application. A second facet, though, might be that this concept requires ensuring that a sufficient proportion of one's forces, relative to the adversary, are employed, so as to enhance the probability of winning. Thus there is a built-in tension between the need for "enough," but not "too much", force. Finally, the term is often used to mean response in kind, or in a tit-for-tat fashion.

vi) *More good than harm*: This is a concept from the Thomist paradigm. This notion implies, of war-fighting, that ethical conduct requires calculation of the net good to be achieved

> by a particular use of force. An example of such a calculation, though clouded by violation of notions of non-combatant immunity, is Truman's decision to drop the atomic bomb on Hiroshima to avoid a more costly conventional invasion of Japan.

IW is demonstrating a growing disruptive capacity, both against classic military command and control nodes and against many elements of the national information infrastructure. A well-informed ethical approach to the burgeoning problem of IW may even demonstrate that it is possible, in this case, to do good and to do well. Indeed, an ethical approach to conflict in the information realm may swiftly prove as practically useful and valuable—even when the opponent is a non-state criminal or terrorist organisation—as it is morally desirable. To consider the ethical dimensions of IW, it is crucial that the phenomenon of IW to be classifiable as a true form of war, as opposed to being just a manifestation of criminal or terrorist activity—or an extension of covert psychological operations or intelligence-oriented activities. In the several years since the introduction of IW, the concept has evolved and broadened to include activities that, while information-driven, are not considered warfare and therefore do not invoke the ethical concepts of just war theory.

To separate these two classes of activities, a broad view has emerged, in which the term information operations refers to the entire range of information-intensive interactions across a spectrum that includes psychological operations; perception management; information security; and, of course, IW. Use of 'information operations' thus allows us to reserve the term IW for a specific subset of warlike activities, all of which invoke just war theory. Principally, this form of war concerns striking at communication nodes and infrastructures.

The weapons used in such attacks are generally thought to be those employable via cyberspace. However, IW also includes the use of a variety of other offensive tools, from conventional explosives to high-power microwave weapons, that can also be used to strike at information-rich targets. Attacks on information-rich targets using conventional weapons, while undoubtedly an integral part of IW, present few ethical novelties because they have long been a part of warfare.

The range of operations that might make use of IW extends broadly, from the battlefield to the enemy home front. Thus, IW may serve as a form of close support for military forces during active operations. It may also be employed in strategic campaigns designed to strike directly at the will and logistical support of an opponent. The last notion of IW, in which it may be pursued without a prior need to defeat an adversary's armed forces, is an area of particular interest. In many respects, it resembles notions of the strategic uses of airpower that emerged in the 1920s and 1930s and merits, therefore, close scrutiny from an ethical perspective.

IW has a quite different set of effects and properties, although it may bear a strategic resemblance to airpower. While airpower can generally perform much destruction on fixed points, information attacks, even using conventional weapons, inflict far less destruction. Rather, the effects of information attacks are disruptive, and may occur over wide areas, even in the face of defensive redundancies emplaced in anticipation of IW attacks. Another difference is that, while strategic aerial bombardment inevitably causes civilian losses, even with today's guided weapons, information weapons will lead to far fewer deaths, despite the widespread disruptive effects. This lower lethality and destructiveness may make the damage done by IW attacks somewhat harder to assess accurately and may complicate calculations designed to craft a proportional response.

Strategic information weapons have area effects that, in some respects, extend quite a bit further than even weapons of mass destruction—but with "mass disruption" being their hallmark. It is just this prospect of having wide effects without causing very many deaths or dire environmental consequences that makes IW such a potentially attractive form of conflict. In strategic aerial bombardment, it is quite clear who is making the attacks. It is also clear that the enemy combatants are its military forces. This latter notion is relaxed a bit in guerrilla warfare, in which civilians often engage in the fighting. But in IW, almost anyone can engage in the fighting. Thus, it is important, from an ethical perspective, to make a distinction between those with access to advanced information technology and those using it for purposes of waging IW. Further, the nature of cyberspace-based attacks is such that there may often be an observational equivalence between criminal, terrorist, and military actions. The ethical imperative that attaches to these concerns is the need to determine the identity of the perpetrators of IW attacks and to make a distinction between sporadic depredations and actions that form part of a recognisable campaign in pursuit of discernible aims.

With the six tenets of just war theory and the pared-down definition of IW, one can relate them each other to determine the extent to which IW can be said to be just or can be waged justly. In the realm of going to war ethically, the concept of "right purpose" does not appear to be put under much stress. Self-defence and pre-emption, both allowed under classical just war theory, may have new dimensions because of IW, as they may be applied more promptly with disruptive information weapons.

The one area that may change is that of the use of force in preventive ways. Under existing just war theory, prevention lies on tenuous ground. But IW might prove especially useful in derailing the rise of a threatening power—particularly the forms of information attack that might be useful in slowing down a potential adversary's process of proliferation of weapons of mass destruction.

Regard to 'duly constituted authority', the second concept of just war theory, the very nature of information weaponry may introduce new stresses for this long-established ethical concept. For the types of capabilities needed to field an IW campaign—particularly one that is waged principally in cyberspace—there is little need for the levels of forces required in other forms of war. Therefore, the state monopoly on war reflected in the concept of duly constituted authority will likely be shaken, as non-state actors rise in their ability to wage IW. This may be part of an overall phenomenon in which the information revolution is causing a diffusion of power away from states and toward non-state actors—both peaceful, civil society elements and the new "uncivil society" of Information Age terrorists and transnational criminal organisations.

This rise of new non-state actors capable of waging IW may also encourage states to employ them. Indeed, non-state actors will likely prove useful cutouts that help to maintain deniability, or ambiguity, about the ultimate identity of an adversary. This suggests the possibility that quite weak states may thus be allowed to strike at the strong, given the lessened likelihood that they will be discovered and subjected to retaliation. However, this problem might be mitigated by improvements in cyberspace-based detection, surveillance, and tracking technologies. This ease of entry into the realm of IW not only erodes the strictures against acting without duly constituted authority.

For IW, though it may disrupt much, at great cost to the target, does little actual destruction—and will likely prove a form of warfare that results in only incidental loss of life. In this respect, IW can be viewed as somewhat akin to economic sanctions as a tool of coercion. This similarity should also contribute to the erosion of the last-resort principle. However, as with economic sanctions, certain non-lethal parts of IW may not be considered acts of war and thus may be exempt from just war considerations—a status that would increase the likelihood of their use but would preserve the integrity of the last-resort principle for actions deemed acts of war. In the case that all IW actions are considered acts of war, if IW's low destructiveness is coupled with a situation that features self-defensive "right purpose"—say, in a crisis where skilful pre-emption might head off a general war—the normative inhibition against early uses of force will erode even further.

With regard to the issue of waging IW justly, there are also many ways in which the classical concepts will come under pressure. First, one approach to IW concentrates on striking an adversary's transportation, power, communication, and financial infrastructures. This must be seen as a kind of war that targets non-combatants in a deliberate manner, because they will suffer from such attacks inevitably and seriously. The purpose of this type of IW is to undermine the enemy's will to resist, or to persist, in a particular fight; in this respect, strategic IW is very similar to early notions of strategic aerial bombardment that targeted non-combatants.

In the realm of IW, even as planners may be driven to wage a form of war whose effects will be most felt by non-combatants, there is another aspect to strategic attack—one strictly aimed at disrupting the movements and operations of military forces. IW is a sufficiently discriminate tool that making this distinction is possible—and just war theory implies eschewing the targeting of non-combatants and focusing instead upon purely military targets and effects. Thus, an apparently quite attractive coercive tool of force runs hard up against the enduring ethical constraints against attacking non-combatants. This dimension of just war theory may, therefore, pose the most nettlesome policy dilemma—and may require the most creative solution. Another thorny issue is posed by the just war-fighting concept of proportionality, whose major concern is with avoiding the use of excessive force during a conflict. In one respect, the discriminate use of IW should make it possible to wage war quite proportionately.

However, two problems might emerge that put notions of proportionality under some stress. First, IW attackers might strike at an opponent's critical infrastructures, but have few of their own that could be retaliated against by means of IW. This prompts the question of when more traditional military measures—including some amount of lethal force—might be used in response to IW attacks without violating notions of proportionality. Another problem might arise if the defender, or target, were struck by IW attack and had little or no means of responding with information weaponry. Aside from deliberately disproportionate responses, there is also the problem that gauging the comparability of damage done by radically differing weapon systems is going to prove quite difficult. The problem of perpetrator ambiguity further weakens proportionate response, because one may simply not have enough data to determine just who is responsible for a particular attack.

The ethical problem deepens when it is recognised that preventive war striking forcefully before an adversary has serious, threatening capabilities will generally mean going to war before diplomatic options have been exhausted, that is, not as a last resort. On the other hand, the basically disruptive rather than destructive nature of IW suggests the possibility of a "just warfighting" approach to prevention that eases the ethical dilemma. Prevention by means of IW might be allowable if:

i) strikes were aimed strictly at military targets, to avoid or generally limit damage to non-combatants;
ii) the good done by preventing an adversary from being able to start a particular conflict, or type of conflict, could be said to outweigh the wrong of using force beyond the realm of clearly definable self-defence.

IW now makes preventive war far more thinkable, straining the limits of the concept of "right purpose". And the manner in which the information revolution empowers small groups and individuals to wage IW suggests that the notion of duly constituted authority may also have lost meaning. Given the ease with which entry may be made into the ranks of IW-capable states and non-state actors and the attractiveness of targets that primarily serve civilian commercial, transportation, financial, resource, and power infrastructures, the greatest *jus in bello* concern for IW may be the problem of maintaining 'non-combatant immunity'. The number of actors will be large and is hardly subject to centralised control. The civilian-oriented target set is huge and is likely to be more vulnerable than the related set of military infrastructures—except to the extent that the infrastructures simultaneously serve both the military and civilian sectors. Thus, the urge to strike at targets that will damage civilians may prove irresistible.

Strategic IW appears to lie somewhere between airpower and economic sanctions on the spectrum of tools of suasion. It can be far more disruptive and costly to an adversary than an economic embargo but is less destructive than bombing characteristics that may make it a very attractive policy option. But the ease of engaging in and the attractiveness of IW must be weighed, for the purpose of policy analysis, against both the ethical and practical concerns.

A significant aspect of IW aims at civilian and civilian-oriented targets; also, despite its negligible lethality, it none the less violates the principle of non-combatant immunity, given that civilian economic or other assets are deliberately targeted. In addition to the ethical dilemma posed by IW, there is the practical problem that whoever might begin the business of striking at civilian-oriented targets would be inviting retaliation in kind—both from nation-states and from individuals or small groups that are armed with advanced information technology.

The discriminate nature of IW should allow a very careful calibration of effects. The only likely difficulty could ensue in situations in which IW attacks do not have the coercive results envisioned. If IW were used preventively or pre-emptively and failed in its purpose, it might even be said that an escalation to general war was the fault of taking the information-warfare action in the first place.

IW and International Law

IW challenges existing international law in three primary ways. First, the sort of intangible damage that such attacks may cause may be analytically different from the physical damage caused by traditional warfare. The kind of destruction that bombs and bullets cause is easy to see and understand, and fits well within longstanding views of what war means. In contrast, the disruption of information systems, including the corruption or manipulation of stored or transmitted data, may cause intangible damage, such as disruption of civil society or government services that may be more closely equivalent to activities such as economic sanctions that may be undertaken in times of peace.

Second, the ability of signals to travel across international networks or through the atmosphere as radio waves challenges the concept of national, territorial sovereignty. Sovereignty, which has been a fundamental principle of international law since the Treaty of Westphalia of 1648, holds that each nation has exclusive authority over events within its borders. Sovereignty may not be suited to an increasingly networked, or "wired" world, as signals travelling across networks or as electromagnetic waves may cross international borders quickly and with impunity, allowing individuals or groups to affect systems across the globe, while national legal authority generally stops at those same borders. Furthermore, the intangible violation of borders that signals may cause may not be the sort of violation traditionally understood to be part of a military attack.

Third, just as IW attacks may be difficult to define as "peace" or "war", it may be hard to define their targets as military or civilian. Furthermore, the intangible damage the attacks cause may not be the sort of injuries against which the humanitarian law of war is designed to protect non-combatants.

The first dilemma that a country that has suffered an information attack may face in responding to the attack may be to identify an event as an actual attack. Especially when an attack does not come during a period of heightened international tensions, it may be difficult for investigators to distinguish a catastrophe resulting from a "natural" or "accidental" computer error from one stemming from malice.

Physical attacks should be distinguishable from accidents or malfunctions, as the culprits must come into some proximity with their target, and they may leave some physical evidence behind.

Computer-based attacks may be even harder to distinguish from innocent malfunctions. If the attack is carried out across a network, the culprits may never be physically close to the target, and they may leave no tangible evidence. Attacks or sabotage using viruses, logic bombs, or simply buggy software may be particularly difficult to detect quickly, if at all, because of the complexity of systems and the frequency of unintentional errors in publicly shipped products.

Software errors or conflicts are known or suspected to have caused a number of incidents that might have seemed to be intentional attacks on important systems, products, or weapons by criminals, terrorists, or even enemy nations.

An incident during a time of heightened international tensions might seem to present evidence that wrongdoing is afoot. Nevertheless, such evidence might not be compelling alone, as times of stress are also the times when complex, brittle systems may be most likely to break down.

Investigators tracing attacks across computer networks may be stymied by a collision between fundamental principles of physics and those of international law, namely, that electrons may flow through networks freely across international borders, but the authority of agents of national governments does not.

Simply, an attack may come from a foreign country, or may be routed through computers in several countries, but law enforcement or national security personnel cannot unilaterally launch pursuit into networks in other countries. Under the principle of sovereignty each government has exclusive authority over events within its borders. Investigators will thus need foreign cooperation or help in their investigations or, with proper domestic authorisation, they will need to operate covertly.

Although the principles of sovereignty were conceived when international law contemplated only physical intrusions into a nation's borders, national governments would probably try to apply the principles to intrusions into computers, networks, or data banks, and they would probably succeed.

Individual governments have already exerted authority over information in domestic systems just as they would if it had physical form; many European governments, as well as the European Union, for example, have enacted data protection codes that forbid the transport or transmission of certain personal data to countries that do not provide sufficient protection for that data. Governments may thus go so far as to consider the act of investigation by foreigners of criminal misuse of their systems to be a form of computer crime, or worse.

Although the stronger view is probably that government agents' intrusion into a foreign computer would constitute a violation of the target nation's sovereignty, it is important to note that not all electronic crossing of boundaries is considered that way. For example, orbital remote sensing, including the bouncing of such signals as radar off a country's territory, is now so universally accepted that it is conducted by private entities, which may sell the products of their sensing on the open market.

Further complicating nations' attempts to trace attacks against them is the international investigatory legal regime, or lack thereof. First, in the absence of a treaty, countries have no underlying obligation to cooperate with each other in their law enforcement or national security investigations. The mere fact of non-cooperation probably cannot be considered evidence of implication in the attack. Even where they had no involvement in, or sympathy for, an attack, hostile or indifferent nations may be unwilling to assist foreign investigators, whom they may view as spies. Even largely friendly governments may be reluctant to cooperate, often for domestic political reasons.

International law enforcement agreements may not be adequate to support an investigation. For example, treaties of mutual legal assistance, which may institutionalise cooperation between countries' law enforcement agencies, generally contain exceptions that permit parties to refuse cooperation under certain circumstances, such as to protect "sovereignty, security, or similar essential interests".In the context of computers, networks, and databases that may implicate a country's national security interests, its technological development, security of its financial and communications infrastructure, or the privacy of its citizens, and where governments may not feel confident about their ability to monitor foreign investigators' activities, some nations may likely at least consider taking advantage of any loopholes they can.

Till today, no provision of international law explicitly prohibits what we now know as IW. This absence of prohibitions is significant because, as a crudely general rule, that which international law does not prohibit it permits. But the absence is not dispositive, because even where international law does not purport to address particular weapons or technologies, its general principles may apply to the use of those weapons and technologies. Nevertheless, existing international law leaves space for many types of IW techniques in many circumstances. Any attack involving networks and telecommunications may implicate the International Telecommunication Union (ITU) and its underlying charter, the International Telecommunication Convention (ITC), which apply to international wire and radio frequency communications.

In practice, the ITU may not substantially limit IW activities, particularly by the United States and especially in a wartime context. The primary concerns of the ITU are interoperability and interference. Its predecessor organisation, the International Telegraph Union, was established in 1865 to facilitate international telegraph traffic, mainly within Europe.

One of the Union's early sets of regulations for radio required interoperability of maritime radio systems, after several dangerous naval incidents occurred because the Marconi Wireless Company, which held the exclusive right to install and operate shipboard radio equipment, refused to permit its operators to communicate with any station that did not use Marconi equipment.

The ITU and the regulations promulgated under it do have some applicability to IW attacks that use the electromagnetic spectrum or international telecommunication networks. First, broadcasting stations from one nation may not interfere with broadcasts of other states' services on their authorised frequencies.

The International Frequency Regulation Board (IFRB) of the ITU allocates the electromagnetic spectrum to prevent interference. Even military installations must observe the non-interference requirement. Additionally, offshore radio stations are banned, and states may not carry out the transmission of false or misleading signals. Finally, governments must protect the secrecy of international correspondence, although they retain the right to stop radio or wire transmissions for national or domestic security purposes.

The IFRB is more of a coordinating body than a regulatory agency, and it has no actual authority to enforce its decisions; rather, countries respect its edicts against interference so that their own communications will be similarly protected.

Even if international sanctions appeared likely, the United States might decide that the risks it faced from external interference would not outweigh its need to conduct operations against a particular adversary. Finally, it is important to note that even where IW activities do violate the ITU or its regulations, mere violations are more likely to be considered breaches of contractual obligations under treaty than acts of war justifying forceful responses.

Interestingly, the Charter of the United Nations, drafted 50 years ago, appears to contemplate such interference with a country's communications as "infoblockades". Article 41 provides that in its effort to address breaches of the peace, the UN Security Council may call upon UN members to disrupt an aggressor's "rail, sea, air, postal, telegraphic, radio, and other means of communication."

Due to the importance of satellites for international telecommunications, as well as for military command, control, communications, and intelligence, many IW attacks may involve orbital assets, and thus implicate space law. Space law, though, leaves ample room for IW.

The fundamental document of space law, the multilateral 1967 Treaty on Principles Governing the Activities of States in the Exploration and Use of Outer Space, including the Moon and Other Celestial Bodies, provides that all states shall be free to explore and use outer space on a basis of equality and that no state may place into earth orbit any objects carrying nuclear weapons or any other kind of "weapon of mass destruction". The 1979 Agreement Concerning the Activities of States on the Moon and Other Celestial Bodies applies similar prohibitions to the moon, and also states that the moon shall only be used for peaceful purposes.

The 1971 Agreement Relating to the International Telecommunications Satellite Organisation (INTELSAT) and the 1976 Convention on the International Maritime Satellite Organisation (INMARSAT) also affect telecommunications and the use of space, but their relevance is limited to principles of non-discrimination among nations using the relevant satellites. None of these conventions bars IW activities that make use of satellite assets.

Despite the novelty of some IW techniques, international law poses some constraints on the conduct of IW, just as it does on the traditional forms of warfare that use kinetic force for their impact. Nevertheless, characteristics of information technology and warfare pose problems to those who would use international law to limit IW, and leave legal space for those who would wage such warfare.

By treaty as well as by longstanding customary law, the territory of neutral states is supposed to be inviolable by the forces of belligerents. Apparently, then, an attack through a network that crosses neutral territory, or using a neutral country's satellites, computers, or networks, would infringe upon that neutral's territory, just as would an overflight by a squadron of bombers or an incursion by armed troops. The attack would thus be considered illegal and, perhaps, an act of war against the neutral. Conversely, a neutral's failure to resist the use of its networks for attacks against another country may make it a legitimate target for reprisals by the country that is the ultimate target of the attacks.

Although the argument that electronic incursion would violate neutrality is strong, a counter-argument exists. The encroachments beyond a nation's borders that may violate its neutrality have, in the past, been physical intrusions by troops, ships, or planes. Attacking a neutral's networks, satellites, or computers might not violate the state's neutrality because it might involve no physical encroachment. Significantly, although neutrals must not allow any belligerent to move troops or supplies through their territory, or to erect military radio stations there, neutrals have no such obligation to prevent belligerents from using their publicly accessible communications equipment.

Despite an unambiguous rule to the contrary, belligerents have quite significantly violated prohibitions against the erection and use of non-public military communications facilities in neutral territory for military purposes. Thus, the vitality of rules regarding neutrals and telecommunications may have been weakened, as countries have acted as if those laws did not, in fact, have legal force.

International humanitarian law would seem to welcome the non-lethal "combat" that IW promises, but that body of law, which is a combination of conventions and longstanding customary law, may constrain IW activities as it does traditional warfare. The fundamental principle of this body of law is that the permissible methods of hurting an enemy are not unlimited, and that the cruelty of war must be mitigated and circumscribed. Nevertheless, although that principle unquestionably survives, even if it is sometimes honoured only in the breach, it is not obvious that all types of damage that information attacks would inflict are the kinds of injuries against which humanitarian law endeavours to protect.

International law has not yet resolved ambiguities over the characterisation of IW activities, and must face a conflict between the international system of sovereign states and the realities of global networks. International law thus leaves space for the United States and others to conduct IW activities, perhaps even in peacetime, without significant legal repercussions.

As the United States apparently leads the world in IW development, an international legal regime that permits information attacks can give it an advantage, allowing the United States to apply its technological strength to international conflicts in ways beyond the capacities of anyone else. In the absence of conclusive legal authority indicating, say, that particular IW attacks are "armed attacks", "aggression", or "force", the United States can act with some confidence that its acts will not be held to be so. Given its position in the world, the United States will have the opportunity to begin the state practice that can establish international norms and, perhaps, customary international law.

To improve its defensive or responsive options, efforts could be made to reconcile the system of sovereign states with international networks, through promoting harmonisation of laws and cooperation in investigation and prosecution of computer attacks. The first part of such a strategy would include diplomatic pressure and criminal justice advice and assistance to promote the criminalisation of computer-based attacks in those nations that do not yet recognise such attacks as crimes, both to encourage other countries to discourage such behaviour by individuals within their borders, and to enable extradition of offenders.

Just as the aviation efforts were incremental steps in the fight against terrorism, similar efforts could be made for the protection of particular information systems from dangers including crime, terrorism, war, or even natural disasters. Some systems may be so critical that countries can agree that they must be put off limits from attacks, or that all countries must cooperate to defend them. Systems that could be the subject of individual protection regimes include those involved in the command and control of strategic weapons, international financial transfers, individual financial markets or stock exchanges, telephone switches, emergency communications, rail transport, and medical databases. Such arrangements could be pursued under direct UN auspices.

An IW weapons ban would pose problems because not only do many information weapons have dual military and civilian uses, but their applications are predominantly civilian. Due to technological diffusion, the small size of much information technology, and its primary incorporation into consumer goods, an arms control regime would seem difficult to enforce.

Although international law does not now conclusively address the legality of many IW attacks or the appropriate responses to them, that has not been a grave problem yet, because the attacks, aside from some computer intrusions and crimes, have not been particularly serious. But as information technology continues to develop and diffuse, the danger of such attacks seems likely only to increase.

REFERENCES

Aldrich, Richard W., "The International Legal Implications of Information Warfare", *INSS Occasional Paper 9, Information Warfare Series*, Colorado Springs: US Air Force Academy, Institute for National Security Studies, April 1996.

Johnson, Deborah G., and Helen Nissenbaum, eds., *Computers, Ethics and Social Values*, Englewood Cliffs, N.J.: Prentice Hall, 1995.

Russell, Frederick H., *The Just War in the Middle Ages*, Cambridge, England: Cambridge University Press, 1975.

Schwartau, Winn, "Ethical Conundra of Information Warfare," in Alan D. Campen, Douglas H. Dearth, and R. Thomas Goodden, eds., *Cyberwar: Security, Strategy and Conflict in the Information Age*, Fairfax, Va.: AFCEA International Press, 1996, pp. 243–249.

Sun Tzu, *The Art of War,* trans. Samuel B. Griffith, Oxford University Press, 1963. Cebrowski, Vice Admiral Arthur K., and John J. Garstka, "Network-Centric

Walzer, Michael, *Just and Unjust Wars,* New York: Basic Books, 1977.

Bibliography

Aldrich, Richard W., "The International Legal Implications of Information Warfare", *INSS Occasional Paper 9, Information Warfare Series*, Colorado Springs: US Air Force Academy, Institute for National Security Studies, April 1996.

Altschiller, Donald (ed.), *The Information Revolution*, New York: Wilson, 1995.

Anthony, Keith D., "Information Warfare: Good News and Bad News", *Military Intelligence* 23, January-March 1997, pp. 31-34.

Arquilla, John, and David F. Ronfeldt, "Cyberwar Is Coming", *Comparative Strategy*, Vol. 12, No. 2, pp. 141–165, RAND, RP-223, Summer 1993.

______________ , *The Advent of Netwar,* Santa Monica, Calif.: RAND, MR-789-OSD, 1996.

Ashman, Bruce W., "Defensive Information Warfare in Today's Joint Operations: What's the Real Threat?", *Strategy Research Project*, Carlisle Barracks: US Army War College, 7 April 1997.

Barac, Gregory G., "Interoperability: The Cornerstone of Information Warfare", *Strategy Research Project*, Carlisle Barracks: US Army War College, 12 April 1996.

Biddle, Stephen, "Assessing Theories of Future Warfare", paper presented to the 1997 Annual Meeting of the American Political Science Association, August 29, 1997, pp. 24–33.

Bob Gelman, Stanton McCandlish, *Protecting Yourself Online: The Definitive Resource on Safety, Freedom, and Privacy in Cyberspace*, HarperCollins Publishers, Incorporated, February 1998.

Borchgrave, Arnaud de, et al., "Cyber Threats and Information Security: Meeting the 21st Century Challenge", Center for Strategic and International Studies, Washington, D.C., December 2000.

Buchan, G. C., *One-and-a-Half Cheers for the Revolution in Military Affairs*, Santa Monica, Calif, 1997.

Campen, Alan D., Douglas H. Dearth, and R. Thomas Goodden, (eds.), *Cyberwar: Security, Strategy, and Conflict in the Information Age*, Fairfax, Va.: AFCEA International Press, 1996.

Cheswick, W. R., and S. M. Bellovin, *Firewalls and Internet Security: Repelling the Wily Hacker,* Addison-Wesley, 1994.

Cohen, Eliot, "A Revolution in Warfare", *Foreign Affairs*, Vol. 75, No. 2, March–April 1996, pp. 46–48.

Computer Science and Telecommunication Board, National Research Council, *Cyber Security Today and Tomorrow: Pay now or Pay Later*, National Academy Press, Washington DC, 2002.

Cook, Wyatt C., "Information Warfare: A New Dimension in the Application of Air and Space Power", *Selected Essays- Air War College Class of 1994,* Maxwell AFB, AL: June 1994.

Cooper, Pat, "Information Warfare Sparks Security Affairs Revolution", *Defense News* 10, pp.1, 66, 12-18 June 1995.

Dearth, Douglas H., "Information War: Rethinking the Application of Power in the 21st Century", *Military Intelligence* 23, pp.11-16, January-March 1997.

Dearth, Douglas, and Charles Williams, "Information Age/Information War", in Campen, Dearth, and Goodden, 1996.

Definitions for the Discipline of Information Warfare and Strategy, Washington, D.C.: School of Information Warfare and Strategy, National Defense University.

Denning, Dorothy E., and William E. Baugh, Jr., *Encryption and Evolving Technologies As Tools of Organized Crime and Terrorism,* Washington, D.C.: U.S. Working Group on Organized Crime (WGOC), National Strategy Information Center, 1997.

Denning, P. J., *Computers Under Attack: Intruders, Worms, and Viruses*, Addison-Wesley, 1990.

Denning, Peter J., (ed.), *Computers under Attack: Intruders, Worms, and Viruses,* Addison Wesley Longman, Inc., January 1990.

Department of Defense. *Information Warfare*, DOD Directive TS3600.1. Washington DC: 21 December 1992.

Department of the Air Force, *Cornerstones of Information Warfare*, Washington, D.C.: Department of the Air Force, 1995.

Department of the Air Force, *Cornerstones of Information Warfare*, Washington, D.C.: Department of the Air Force, 1995.

Department of the Navy, *Policy Planning and Guidance for Naval Information Warfare/Command and Control Warfare.*, Washington DC: 16 Feb. 1995.

Edward, Taylor, B., "Building a Minefield Database System", *Engineer* 26, pp.14-16, December 1996.

FBIS, "Arab Afghans Said to Launch Worldwide Terrorist War", *Paris al-Watan al-'Arabi*, December 1, pp. 22–24, 1995.

Friedman, George, and Meredith Friedman, *The Future of War: Power, Technology and American World Dominance in the 21st Century*, New York: St Martin's Press, 1997.

Grimes, Roger A. A., Sue Miller (eds.), *Malicious Mobile Code: Virus Protection for Windows*, O'Reilly & Associates, Incorporated, August 2001.

Hansen, M. H., *Modern Methods for Computer Security and Privacy*, Prentice-Hall, 1977.

Harknett, Richard J., "Information Warfare and Deterrence", *Parameters*, Autumn 1996, pp. 93–107.

Hatch, Brian, James Lee, George Kurtz, *Hacking Linux Exposed: Linux Security Secrets and Solutions*, McGraw-Hill Professional Book Group, April 2001.

Hoffman, Bruce, "Responding to Terrorism Across the Technological Spectrum", in John Arquilla and David Ronfeldt, eds., *In Athena's Camp: Preparing for Conflict in the Information Age*, Santa Monica, Calif.: RAND, pp. 339–367, 1997.

Hopper, William Frank., *Command and Control Countermeasures Doctrine in the Naval Environment*, Monterey, CA: Naval post-graduate School, June 1983.

Howard, John D., *An Analysis of Internet Security Incidents, 1989–1995.* unpublished dissertation., Pittsburgh, Penn.: Carnegie Mellon University, 1997.

Hundley, Richard O., and Robert H. Anderson, "Emerging Challenge: Security and Safety in Cyberspace", *IEEE Technology and Society Magazine,* Vol. 14, No. 4, pp. 19–28, Winter 1995–1996.

Hutcherson, Norman B., *Command and Control Warfare*, Maxwell AFB, Alabama: Air University Press, 1994.

Johnson, Deborah G., and Helen Nissenbaum, eds., *Computers, Ethics and Social Values*, Englewood Cliffs, N.J.: Prentice Hall, 1995.

Keegan, John, *The Second World War,* New York: Viking, 1989.

Kurlantzick, Joshua, "Muslim Separatists in Global Network of Terrorist Groups", *Washington Times*, May 2, 2000.

Libicki, Martin C., *What Is Information Warfare?* Washington, D.C.: National Defense University, 1995.

____________, *Defending Cyberspace and Other Metaphors*, Washington, D.C.: NDU Books, 1997.

Mahnken, Thomas G., "War in the Information Age", *Joint Forces Quarterly*, pp. 39–43, Winter 1995–1996.

McClure, Stuart, George Kurtz, *Hacking Exposed: Network Security Secrets and Solutions*, Joel Scambray, McGraw-Hill Professional Book Group, October 2000.

Molander, Roger C., Andrew S. Riddile, and Peter A. Wilson, "Strategic Information Warfare: A New Face of War", *Parameters*, Autumn 1996, pp. 81-92.

Morton, Oliver, "Defence Technology: The Information Advantage", *Economist* 335, 10 June 1995.

Murray, Williamson, "Thinking about Revolutions in Military Affairs", *Joint Forces Quarterly,* Summer 1997, pp. 60–76.,

_____________, Allan R. Millett, (ed.), *Military innovation in the Interwar Perio*d, New York: Cambridge University Press, 1996.

Nacos, Brigitte, Nohria, Nitin, and Robert Eccles, eds., *Networks and Organization*s, Boston, Mass.: Harvard Business School Press, 1992.

_____________, *Terrorism and the Media,* New York: Columbia University Press, 1994.

Nichiporuk, Brian, and Carl H. Builder, *Information Technologies and the Future of Land Warfar*e, Santa Monica, Calif.: RAND, MR-560-A, 1995.

Nichiporuk, Brian, and Carl H. Builder, *Information Technologies and the Future of Land Warfar*e, Santa Monica, Calif., 1995.

Northcutt, Stephen, Judy Novak, Donald McLachlan, *Network Intrusion Detection: An Analyst's Handbook*, New Riders Publishing, September 2000.

Nye, Joseph, and William Owens, "The Information Edge", *Foreign Affair*s, Vol. 75, No. 2, March/April 1996.

Paige, Emmett, Jr., "The Future of Information Security", *Defense Issues* 11, no. 71, pp.1-3, 1996.

Parker, Donna, *Fighting Computer Crime: A New Framework for Protecting Information*, Wiley, John & Sons, Incorporated, August 1998.

Petersen, John L., *Info War: The Next Generation,* Proceedings: U.S. Naval Institute 123, pp.60-62, January 1997.

Potter, David L., "Information Warfare: Malicious Software and Technology", *Military Intelligence* 23, January-March 1997, pp.34-37.

Richardson, Doug, "Information Warfare—New Threats and New Opportunities", *Asian Defence Journal*, no. 4, April 1997, pp.50-55.

Robert Slade, *Robert Slade's GuideTo Computer Viruses: How to Avoid Them, How To Get Rid Of Them And How To Get Help*, Springer-Verlag New York, Incorporated, March 1996.

Rosenblatt, K. S., *High Technology Crime: Investigating Cases Involving Computers*, KSK Publications, San Jose, CA, 1995.

Royal Canadian Mounted Police (RCMP), *Guide to Threat and Risk Assessment for Information Technology*, November, 1994.

Russell, Frederick H., *The Just War in the Middle Ages*, Cambridge, England: Cambridge University Press, 1975.

Ryan, Donald E., Jr., "Implications of Information-Based Warfare", *Joint Force Quarterly*, no. 6, 1994-1995, pp.114-16.

Schmauder, Phil, *Virus Proof: The Ultimate Guide to Protecting Your System with CD-ROM*, Prima Communications, Inc., April 2000.

Schwartau, Winn, "Ethical Conundra of Information Warfare," in Alan D. Campen, Douglas H. Dearth, and R. Thomas Goodden, eds., *Cyberwar: Security, Strategy and Conflict in the Information Age*, Fairfax, Va.: AFCEA International Press, 1996, pp. 243–249.

Schwartau, Winn, *Cybershock: Surviving Hackers, Phreakers, Identity Thieves, Internet Terrorists, and Weapons of Mass Disruption*, Avalon, New York, April 2000.

Schwartau, Winn, *Information Warfare: Chaos on the Electronic Superhighway*, New York: Thunder's Mouth Press, 1994.

Schwartzstein, Stuart J.D., (ed.), *The Information Revolution and National Security: Dimensions and Directions*, Washington: Center for Strategic and International Studies, 1996.

Skardhamar, Rune, *Virus: Detection and Elimination*, Academic Press, Incorporated, October 1995.

Stallings, William, *Network Security Essentials: Applications and Standards*, Prentice Hall PTR, November 1999.

Sterling, Bruce, *The Hacker Crackdown: Law and Disorder on the Electronic Frontier*, Bantam Books, Incorporated, October 1993.

Sun Tzu, *The Art of War,* (trans.), Samuel B. Griffith, Oxford University Press, 1963. Cebrowski, Vice Admiral Arthur K., and John J. Garstka, "Network-Centric

Thomas, Tim, "The Threat of Information Operations: A Russian Perspective", in Robert Pfaltzgraff and Richard Shultz, eds., *War in the Information Age: New Challenges for U.S. Security*, London: Brassey's, 1997.

Toffler, "Onward Cyber Soldiers", *Time Magazine,* August 21, Volume 146, No. 8, 1995.

Toffler Heidi and Alvin, *War and Anti-War: Survival at the Dawn of the Twenty-First Century*, New York: Warner Books, 1993.

Toxen, Bob, *Real World Linux Security: Intrusion Prevention, Detection and Recovery with CD-ROM*, Prentice Hall PTR, November 2000.

Tsymbal, V. I., "Concepts of Information Warfare", a speech presented at the conference on Evolving Post–Cold War National Security Issues, held in Moscow, September 12–14, 1995.

Van Creveld, Martin, *The Transformation of War*, New York: Free Press, 1991.

Waller, Douglas, "Onward Cyber Soldiers", *Time,* August 21, 1995.

Walzer, Michael, *Just and Unjust Wars,* New York: Basic Books, 1977.

Ward, Robert W., et al. "C3/Space and Electronic Warfare", *Desert Storm Reconstruction Report*, vol. VIII, Alexandria, VA: Center for Naval Analysis. June 1992.

Warden, Col. John A. *The Air Campaign: Planning For Combat*, Washington, DC: National Defense University Press, 1988.

Weible, Jack, "Vulnerable to Attack? Subcommittees Get an Earful on Threats to Information Systems", *Air Force Times* 57, pp.28, 14 April 1997.

Whine, Michael, "Islamist Organizations on the Internet," *Terrorism and Political Violence*, Vol. 11, No. 1, Spring 1999.

Whitehead, YuLin, "Information as a Weapon: Reality versus Promises", *Airpower Journal* 11, pp.40-54, 1997.

Widnall, Sheila, and Richard Fogleman, "Cornerstones of Information Warfare", U.S. Air Force White Paper, 1996.

Williams, Phil, "Transnational Criminal Organisations and International Security", *Survival*, Vol. 36, No. 1, pp. 96–113, 1994.

Williams, Robert H., "Info Warfare Attacks Score in Military's Risk Pantheon, *National Defense* 81, pp.16-17, September 1996.

Williamson, John, "Winning the Data War", *Jane's Defence Weekly* 23, pp.44-46, 20 May 1995.

Wilson, E., "The Information Revolution and National Security", Draft, Center for International Development and Conflict Management, College Park, Md.: University of Maryland, October 31, 1995.

Index